Abnormal Postural Reflex Activity
Caused by Brain Lesions

Abnormal Postural Reflex Activity Caused by Brain Lesions

BERTA BOBATH, FCSP

Principal,
The Western Cerebral Palsy Centre,
London

Third Edition

 ® AN ASPEN PUBLICATION®
Aspen Systems Corporation
Rockville, Maryland
1985

First published 1965; reprinted 1968, 1969, 1970
Second edition 1971; reprinted 1972, 1974, 1975, 1976, 1978
Third edition (reset) 1985

William Heinemann Medical Books Ltd.
23 Bedford Square, London WC1B 3HH

Library of Congress Cataloging in Publication Data
Bobath, Berta.
Abnormal Postural Reflex Activity caused by Brain Lesions.

'Published in association with The Chartered Society of Physiotherapy'
Bibliography p. 107. Includes Index
1. Brain damage – complications and sequelae. 2. Reflexes, abnormal. 3. Posture disorders.
I. Chartered Society of Physiotherapy (Great Britain)
II. Title. (DNLM: 1. Brain damage, chronic. 2. Reflex, abnormal. WL 340 B663a)

RC 387.5.B63 1985   618.92'83   84-24451

ISBN 0-87189-091-7 (Aspen Systems Corp.)

For information, address Aspen Systems Corporation
                    1600 Research Boulevard, Rockville,
                    Maryland 20850.

Library of Congress Catalog Card Number 84-24451
ISBN 0-87189-091-7

Printed in Great Britain by:
Spottiswoode Ballantyne Printers Ltd., Colchester and London

Also by Berta Bobath:

Motor Development in the Different Types of Cerebral Palsy
William Heinemann Medical Books, London, 1975.

Adult Hemiplegia: Evaluation and Treatment, 2nd edition
William Heinemann Medical Books, London, 1978.

Of related interest:

Occupational Therapy in the Treatment of Adult Hemiplegia
Ortrud Eggers, translated by Christine Diebel, with a Foreword
by Berta and Karel Bobath.
William Heinemann Medical Books, London/Aspen Systems
Corporation, Rockville, Maryland, 1983.

Contents

Preface to Third Edition

The first edition of this book was written in 1965 as a thesis describing the influence of abnormal postural reflex activity on the motor behaviour of patients with upper motor lesions, mainly children with cerebral palsy. At that time spasticity was still regarded as a local phenomenon affecting individual muscles and showing itself in exaggerated stretch reflexes. This view led to local treatment for spastic muscles, such as physiotherapy on orthopaedic lines, i.e. exercises to strengthen weak antagonists of spastic muscle as well as some surgery and bracing. The effect of released tonic reflex activity on the strength and distribution of spasticity over the body muscula- ture was not known, or that spasticity manifests itself in patterns of hypertonus affecting not individual muscles, but involving all the affected parts of the body in widespread patterns of posture and movement.

In order to substantiate this view, a description of various tonic reflexes taken from the publications of Magnus (1924, 1926) Walshe (1923, 1946) and others were – and still are – given in the first part of the book. The influence of the patterns of released tonic reflexes on the motor behaviour of children with cerebral palsy was observed and described. The close interaction of these reflexes was pointed out, as well as the difficulty of interpreting the effect of each one of these simple reflexes on patients.

In the second part of the book, stato-kinetic reactions were described which were based on the publications of Schalten- brand (1925, 1926, 1927), Weisz (1938) and Rademaker (1935). These, in contrast to the tonic reflexes, are normal postural reactions and are part of a child's motor development. They are higher integrated reactions such as the righting and equilibrium reactions, the latter being also called balance reactions. They make normal postural control and movements against gravity possible and are a protection against falling. It was shown that they could not function in children with cerebral palsy due to the dominance of released abnormal tonic reflex activity.

Even in 1965 we realized that the abnormal motor behaviour in children with cerebral palsy could not be explained purely in terms of a few tonic reflexes for the following reasons:

1   They interact in algebraical summation, i.e. strengthen and weaken each other. This makes it impossible to ascribe any one pattern to one or other of the tonic reflexes.

2   In the individual case, especially in the milder ones, we see compensatory and secondary abnormal postural patterns of motor behaviour which cannot be explained by the action of any one reflex.

3   The degree of stimulation, i.e. speed of handling, environmental and emotional stimulation influenced the presence or absence of tonic reflexes at any one time of testing. Only in the most severe cases of spasticity did they occur with some regularity, while in the milder cases and in very young children they only showed themselves under stress.

4   In older cases with contractures already established, the clear patterns of tonic reflexes were changed and their influence could only be inferred.

We have since learned that it was a mistake to apply the neuro-physiological observations derived from animal experiments to human beings who have a much higher developed CNS. It must be kept in mind that many factors other than the few tonic reflexes influence the patterns of hypertonus such as stimulation, effort and compensation.

Nevertheless, in spite of the above, we felt that the description of the interplay of these original reflex patterns serves to explain the abnormal motor behaviour of children with cerebral palsy to some extent.

At the time of writing the first edition, we felt that testing for individual tonic reflexes would be useful in assessing a child's condition, helping diagnosis and even treatment. However, other workers used, and still use, testing procedures of single reflexes on the basis of our publications: Koeng (1962), Matthias (1966), Flehmig (1970), Fiorentino (1973), Capute *et al.* (1978), Vojta (1981), Knupfer and Rathke (1982).

We have abandoned such tests for many years because they have not proved helpful in the assessment and planning of treatment. In fact, it has led to 'the treatment of reflexes' rather than of children. Instead, we now test for the individual reactions of patterns of hypertonus and their interference with normal activity.

In keeping with the publications available to us in 1965 and 1971, we used the term 'reflexes' rather loosely. However, we now accept Sherrington's view that a reflex is a stereotyped response, always recurring in the same unchanging manner, requiring an adequate stimulus applied with the receptive field of any particular reflex.

Because of the great variability of the above mentioned postural reactions the use of the term 'postural reflexes', when applied to the motor behaviour of children and adults, now seems to us increasingly questionable. Even the tonic reflex patterns seen in patients with spasticity are so variable and the higher organized righting and balance reactions are yet more so, that one should rather talk about 'postural reactions' or 'responses'.

In the publications of Magnus, Schaltenbrand, Walshe *et al.*, on which this book is based, the term 'reflex' appears at times alternating with 'reaction'. In writing the third edition, when quoting from the original texts of more recent writers the reader will find an even greater variety of terms used for the same type of response—such as reflexes, primitive reflexes, reactions and responses. Not only do the individual authors use different terms but the same author may alternate between them in the same paper. The ambiguous use of these terms already presented some difficulties in the second edition when quoting other workers. For instance on page 60 a footnote was added which said: 'In this and subsequent chapters the word "reflex" is used in conformity with the usage of Magnus, Schaltenbrand and other writers, upon which this work is based, but the term "reaction" would be more appropriate to describe the responses discussed.'

Many workers are now testing asymmetrical and symmetrical tonic reflexes and tonic labyrinthine reflexes on babies at risk under the age of 4 months. However, what the examiner may see occasionally in these babies as transient postural patterns is nothing else than the shadow of the influence of primitive phylogenetic patterns before higher centres mature and modify these early patterns. Hirt (1967) has tried to prove that even in normal adults tonic reflexes, such as the asymmetrical tonic neck reflex, are present. Again, the fact that extensor tonus increased with voluntary effort in the subject's face-arm and flexor tonus in the skull-arm, as demonstrated with EMG findings, does not mean that these were 'reflexes' but, as in the normal baby, transient shadows of patterns of lower integration when tonus increased under stress. Such increases of tonus in the normal baby or adult does not interfere with the normal variety of movement since it occurs as the result of released and obligatory reflex activity.

In the years between the first and third edition of this book, a great deal of research has been undertaken on the study of the motor development of normal babies, describing new test procedures of early responses in the neonatal period and their changes in the maturing baby. Some of these were included in the second edition; a more complete list of early reactions and their gradual modification is added in this third edition as a means of detecting early signs of retardation or pathology.

K. and B. Bobath

This work is the result of an analysis of the motor behaviour of patients with various lesions of the central nervous system. The majority of cases were children suffering from cerebral palsy, i.e. from congenital quadruplegia, spastic diplegia, hemiplegia or paraplegia, some of whom showed mixed symptoms of spasticity and athetosis, athetosis with ataxia, or spasticity with ataxia. A number of cases were adults suffering from cerebral palsy, or of residual hemiplegia due to vascular accident or head injury, while a few were of disseminated sclerosis and Friedreich's ataxia. (The associated pathology should be studied in the appropriate textbooks on Nervous Diseases.)

In previous papers a treatment for children and adults suffering from lesions of the nervous system was described. The problem was seen as a neurophysiological one, and it was stressed that the cause of the motor disability of patients was largely due to the release of abnormal and widespread reflex patterns of posture and movement from the inhibition normally exerted by higher centres of the central nervous system.

The central nervous system acts as a coordinating organ for the multitude of incoming sensory stimuli, producing integrated motor responses adequate to the requirements of the environment. Muscles are grouped in coordinated action patterns, some contracting, some holding and others relaxing. In a critical review of the experimental work on this subject, Walshe (1946) in citing Hughlings Jackson says: 'The cortex knows nothing of muscles, it knows only of movements.'

In the performance of our everyday movements we are not conscious of the function of the individual muscles concerned with the movements, nor can we follow up or direct voluntarily every part of a movement at every stage of it. Kinnier Wilson (1925) says:

> '... "voluntary movements" are not *sui generis* in the sense of constituting a class apart; they are equivalent to "least automatic" movements, and all gradations may occur from "most automatic" to "least automatic".'

A large part of our voluntary movements is automatic and outside consciousness, and this applies especially to the postural adjustment of the various parts of the body which accompany them. For the maintenance of posture and equilibrium, the central nervous system utilises lower centres of integration with their phylogenetically and ontogenetically older patterns of coordination. These centres are in the brainstem, cerebellum, midbrain and basal ganglia.

The release of motor responses integrated at these lower levels from the restraining influence of higher centres, especially that of the cortex, leads to abnormal postural reflex activity. For an understanding of the movement disorders of patients with lesions to the CNS, it is essential to realise that damage to the CNS results in abnormal coordination of muscle action and not in paralysis of muscles. The released abnormal patterns of posture are typical and stereotyped, and they involve all the muscles of the affected parts or of the whole body. They are largely responsible for the typical picture of the patient's postures and movements.

Abnormal postural reflexes can be observed only in patients with lesions of the CNS where their release has led to their appearance in an exaggerated form. But even then, it is difficult to isolate the various postural reflexes, as the picture is usually complicated by the simultaneous action of a number of these reflexes and by the patient's volitional efforts when using their patterns for function.

They have been studied in isolation by Sherrington (1947), Magnus (1924, 1926) and other workers on animals with experimentally produced lesions of the CNS.

The motor responses resulting from the action of a group of *normal* postural reactions integrated at subcortical levels have been termed 'principal motility' (Schaltenbrand, 1927). These reactions can be observed in the normal human being and their gradual development studied in babies and young children. They become modified and changed by the activity of higher centres into more complex and more differentiated skilled motor patterns.

The regulation of muscle tone throughout the body for the maintenance of posture and for the performance of movements is the function of the proprioceptive system. Postural reflexes play a dominant role in the regulation of the degree and the distribution of muscle tone. Most of these reflexes are elicited by stimulation of the sensory end organs in the muscles and joints and by the labyrinths (the otoliths and the semicircular canals). Exceptions are those righting reflexes, to be described later, which are elicited by tactile stimulation of the body surface, and the optical righting reflexes. Muscle tone is dependent on an intact proprioceptive reflex arc, its source lying in the muscle itself. The proprioceptive organs are stimulated by movements of the body (Fulton, 1951). Bernstein (1967) says:

> 'The physiological data available on tonus has considerably extended the initial ideas on this topic which at first incorporated only the idea of a condition of elasticity of the muscle fibres. Without any more accurate determinations tonus, in the vocabulary of physiologists began gradually to cover a very wide range of facts beginning with decerebrate rigidity and extending to Magnus and de Klejn's tonus which has already been understood as a very generalized state of the motor periphery of preparation (in particular of the musculature of the neck and body) for the accomplishment of positions or movements.'

The older, static concept of tonus as physiological elasticity constricted and retarded the understanding of these phenomena. It seems that there is at present enough evidence to decide upon a judgment, perhaps preliminary, and to say the following about tonus:

a   Tonus as an ongoing physiological adaptation and

    organization of the periphery is not a condition of elasticity, but a condition of readiness.

b Tonus is not merely a condition of the muscles, but of the entire neuromuscular apparatus, including at least the final spinal synapse and the final common pathways.

c Tonus, from this point of view, is related to coordination as a state is to an action or as a precondition is to an effect.

If taken as working hypotheses these suppositions allow us to explain much more . . .

> 'One is struck by the fact (which was not considered before, but which after these hypotheses are made become quite obvious) that not a single case of pathological coordination is known in which there is not at the same time a pathology of tonus, and that not a single central nervous apparatus is known which is related to one of these functions without being related to the other . . .' (Bernstein, 1967).

Experiments on animals have shown that transection of the neuraxis at different levels produced a different state of muscle tone. Sherrington found that prepontine transection of the brainstem induced a state of exaggerated posture, characterized by continuous spasm of the skeletal muscles, predominantly of the extensors. He termed the phenomenon 'decerebrate rigidity', and regarded it as a 'release phenomenon' due to the interruption of projection fibres from higher levels (Fulton, 1951). This transection was performed below the level of the red nucleus. Transections made at a still lower level, that of the first and second cervical cord, abolished the rigidity and the muscles became flaccid.

    Thus we see that owing to the activity of a reflex mechanism integrated at the level of the brainstem, sustained muscular contractions occur which do not fatigue. Magnus called these reflexes 'tonic' or 'static' reflexes. Their functional significance is the maintenance of posture against gravity (they are absent at the spinal level of integration). Spinal man, as seen in the

paraplegic patient, cannot stand because he lacks the sustained
tone necessary for standing. He shows only phasic reflexes, such
as the flexor withdrawal reflex, the extensor thrust, the crossed
extension reflex and the stepping reflex.

A condition comparable to decerebrate rigidity has been
observed by Walshe (1923) in patients suffering from spastic
hemiplegia, and by Riddoch and Buzzard (1921) in patients
with quadruplegia and hemiplegia. Walshe says:

> 'Neurologists are learning from Sherrington to regard muscle tone
> as the basis of posture, and decerebrate rigidity as a form of reflex
> standing. In the earlier analysis of spasticity, as it occurs in
> hemiplegia and in the extended form of paraplegia, reasons were
> given for regarding it as physiologically identical with experiment-
> ally produced decerebrate rigidity.'

Spasticity in patients is the result of a release of tonic reflex
activity, and if it be severe, it may approximate to decerebrate
rigidity. Sherrington considered decerebrate rigidity to be a
'caricature of standing'. Patients with severe degrees of spasticity can support their body weight when put on their feet, but
they are unable to maintain their balance. For this they need
the function of higher centres which modify and inhibit tonic
reflexes and allow for weightbearing with mobility.

Magnus (1926) has described the changes of muscle tone and
postural behaviour which took place in animals after transection of the neuraxis at a higher level, leaving the red nucleus
and its connections intact. The condition of the animal was then
no longer 'decerebrate', but became normal. Rigidity was
absent, the distribution of tone was normal, and the animal
showed the righting function, which enabled it to right itself by
its own active movements from all abnormal positions, and to
preserve the normal one against all disturbing influences.

This state of normal muscle tone and normal righting ability
in the absence of cortical control does not hold good for man.
Here the development of the cerebral cortex has led to an
inhibition of the activity of subcortical centres. They have lost

their autonomy and become relegated into the background of human motor activity. In the process of evolution man has become dependent on intact cortical activity for the maintenance of the upright posture in standing and walking, and for the complex activities of arms and hands in prehension and skilled movements. A lesion of the brain in man will, therefore, result in greater helplessness than a comparable lesion in an animal. This point is stressed by Fulton (1951) who compares the difference in behaviour of thalamic monkeys and thalamic dogs or cats. He finds that:

'. . . the midbrain dog or cat (with part of the thalamus intact and hence often designated a thalamic animal) has, when on its four feet, normal distribution of postural tone, and is capable of walking, whereas the thalamic monkey has abnormal posture and is quite unable to walk.'

The righting function, which is the result of a group of 'righting reflexes' integrated at the midbrain level, is absent in patients with strong release of tonic reflex activity, the latter producing severe degrees of spasticity. Patients with moderate or slight spasticity, that is to say with more normal muscle tone, usually exhibit righting reflexes. These observations show that there is a relationship between tonic and righting reflexes. If tonic reflexes are hyperactive, i.e. if muscle tone is greatly increased, righting reflexes are absent. They are inhibited by the dominance of abnormally strong tonic reflexes. On the other hand, if righting reflexes are active, they modify and inhibit the tonic reflexes. In doing this they play an essential part in maintaining a muscle tone of moderate intensity, which is of sufficient strength to counteract gravity and to give fixation to movements, but at the same time of sufficiently low intensity to allow for movements to take place easily and freely. (A better term for righting reflexes is righting 'reactions' because they are more variable than reflexes.)

In the first part of this book the tonic or static reflexes are described, and their effect on the patient's motor behaviour discussed. These tonic reflexes are released from higher control and are symptoms of pathology of the CNS in the spastic patient. The second part describes higher postural reflexes, such as the righting reflexes and the equilibrium reactions. They form the background of normal movements and appear in a developmental sequence in the growing child. In treatment of patients with hypertonus, they will reduce spasticity.

The knowledge of the individual reflexes as they are described by Magnus (1924, 1926) enables us to explain some of the motor behaviour of patients and to recognize their influence in the coordination of the patient's typical postures and movements. Though isolated reflexes can hardly ever be seen, since the motor patterns observed are the result of a combination of reflexes acting simultaneously, certain distinct patterns which recur in the same circumstances can be traced to the dominating influence of one or other single postural reflex. It is comparatively easy to note this in severely spastic patients, who show released tonic reflex patterns most clearly. In the less severe cases, especially when under stress, we may see only traces of the typical tonic reflex patterns, because such patients show more varied and higher organized reaction patterns and are often capable of voluntary movements. We may then not be able to elicit the reflexes proper, but will only find their influence in the changing distribution and degree of tonus when we test the resistance to passive movements.

Magnus grouped the static reflexes into local static, segmental static and general static reactions, according to whether they involved one limb, both fore- or hind-limbs, or the whole body.

THE POSITIVE AND NEGATIVE SUPPORTING REACTIONS

Magnus (1926) has shown that by a series of local static reflexes a limb which sometimes moved freely in all joints was at other times transformed into a stiff and strong pillar and able to carry the weight of the body.

The adequate stimulus for this reaction is a twofold one:

1   A proprioceptive stimulus by stretch of muscles produced by dorsiflexion of the distal parts of the limb (fingers, hand, toes and foot).
2   An exteroceptive stimulus evoked by the contact of the pads of the foot with the ground.

The static response ends with the removal of these two stimuli, which occurs when the limb of the standing animal is lifted from the ground. The whole limb then becomes loose in all its joints and free for movement.

Magnus called the process by which the movable limb changed into a stiff pillar the 'positive supporting reaction', and the opposite process of loosening of the limb the 'negative supporting reaction'.

The positive supporting reaction is characterized by the simultaneous contraction of flexors and extensors. The functional grouping of the antagonistic muscles in this reaction differs totally from that taking place in ordinary movements. The antagonists do not relax but contract, exerting a synergic function which results in the fixation of the joints (co-contraction).

The positive supporting reaction is a modification of the

extensor thrust, a spinal reflex described by Sherrington (1947), which consists of a brief extensor reaction, evoked by a stimulus of sudden pressure to the pads of the foot and affecting all of the extensor muscles of the limb with relaxation of their antagonists. Fulton (1951) describes it as 'a fractional manifestation of the positive supporting reaction of Magnus'.

The negative supporting reaction is, according to Magnus, characterized by a reflex relaxation of the extensors of the proximal joints. Thus the whole limb is loosened, especially at the proximal joints, and becomes free for movement.

The positive supporting reaction and its effect on the patient

The influence of the positive supporting reaction can be seen more or less clearly in all spastic patients. Such patients in standing and walking always touch the ground first with the ball of the foot, thus evoking the reaction. As in the experimental animal, the leg becomes immediately stiff by the simultaneous contraction of flexors and extensors. Though the leg in the standing patient becomes rigid, both in hemiplegias and diplegias, we find in the former condition a preponderance of extensor spasticity with a relative inhibition of the flexors and a more extended posture of the leg, whereas in the diplegic patient hypertonicity of the flexors is pronounced and in some cases approximates to that of the extensors. The posture of the legs of the diplegic patient, therefore, shows various degrees of semiflexion at the hip and knee joints, which allied with adductor spasm and internal rotation produces the well-known scissor posture and gait. Certain features, however, are common to the standing posture of all spastic patients. Extension and inversion of the ankle is present so that the heel cannot be brought to the ground; there is also 'clawing' of the toes, which is part of the exaggerated extensor activity; the weight of the body is on the ball of the foot and, in addition to the body weight, there is considerable pressure against the ground. In all types of cases we find inward rotation of the leg at the hip combined, in the case of the diplegic patient, with adductor spasm, while the hemiplegic patient shows exaggerated abductor activity due to backward rotation of the pelvis on the affected side. In both types of patients the attempt to dorsiflex the ankle or flex the knee of the standing leg will be resisted. If one succeeds, however, in doing this, the patient will collapse: he is unable to carry the weight of the body on a flexed leg.

The pillar-like rigidity of the legs in weight-bearing, resulting from the influence of the positive supporting reaction, has the following consequences:

> A rigid limb may carry the weight of the body, but it cannot contribute to any balance reactions which need mobility of the joints and constantly changing fine postural adjustments of the state of the muscles. The difficulty of maintaining and regaining balance is increased by the fact that the supporting base is very small, since only the ball of the foot touches the ground. In the diplegic patient the standing base is further reduced by the adductor spasm. All attempts at maintaining balance have, therefore, to be of a compensatory nature and must come from other parts of the body, as for instance, the trunk, arms and hands, or in the hemiplegic patient from the unaffected side of the body.

Furthermore, extensor spasticity prevents the dorsiflexion of the foot and is responsible for the clawing of the toes. Because of this, most patients find it impossible to place the heel on the ground in standing, and none of them can stand with the weight of the body on the heels, or put the heel down first in walking. Normal weight transference of the body-weight over the standing leg in walking is made impossible because of the patient's inability to achieve the full degree of dorsiflexion of the ankle required for this weight transference.

Extensor spasticity is essential for weight-bearing in the spastic patient; without it he could not stand or walk. But it has the serious disadvantage, among others, of preventing dorsiflexion of the foot. This is generally appreciated, and the operation of lengthening the tendo achilles was devised to give the patient a walking base on the whole foot. It is interesting to compare the results of this operation in different types of patients. In the hemiplegic patient, and in those diplegics with marked extensor spasticity, the artificially produced dorsiflexion of the ankle does not seem to interfere with the extensor activity of the more proximal parts of the leg. However, in those diplegic patients who show both marked flexor and extensor spasticity, lengthening of the tendo achilles often results in a permanent increase of the flexor activity at hip and knee with a severe inhibition of the extensor muscles, producing a flexor deformity at hip, knee and ankle, and in time leading to a calcaneus posture of the foot.

Another example of the harmful influence of the positive supporting reaction can be seen in the patient's inability to move the joints of the leg while weight-bearing, that is, to maintain the standing posture during various degrees of flexion at hip, knee and ankle. This disability shows itself most clearly when the patient tries to get up from a chair, or when he sits down or walks downstairs. When trying to stand up from a chair, the patient pushes with his feet against the ground, the legs become stiff, through the influence of the positive supporting reaction, and he pushes himself backward into the chair. He can only achieve a standing position if he can pull himself forward with his hands; he does not bend his hips or knees in doing so. When he sits down, he falls backward into the chair without bending his legs, as long as they carry his body-weight; he often sits with extended knees. The normal way of getting up from a chair is to bring the body-weight forward on to the dorsiflexed feet by flexing hips and knees and extending the spine. The flexed legs then take the weight of the body and extend afterwards. If the spastic patient is made to do this movement of transferring his body-weight on to his flexed legs, and he is asked to lift himself off the chair in this position, he will collapse and sit on the floor. In walking downstairs, when gradual flexion of the knee of the weight-bearing leg is essential while the other foot descends to the next step, the patient would collapse on the standing leg if he tried to flex it to any degree. He has, therefore, to hold on to the bannister to support his weight. The hemiplegic patient walking downstairs will descend first with the stiffly extended affected leg, while lowering his weight on the sound leg, and then repeat the same procedure instead of alternating his steps.

The negative supporting reaction and its effect on the patient

The reflex relaxation of the extensor muscles at the proximal joints, which sets the standing leg free to move, does not occur in any strength in the spastic patient. The positive supporting reaction never becomes sufficiently inhibited, extensor activity continuing even in the moving leg, which never relaxes completely, although there is a certain reduction of the strength of extensor tone. This cocontraction of flexors and extensors makes it difficult to lift the leg in order to make a step. Both legs remain stiff, not only in standing but also in walking, and the patient cannot lift the moving leg sufficiently off the ground. The reason for this may be that in man, who moves in the upright posture on two legs, extensor activity, especially at the hips, is much more pronounced and less easy to inhibit than that of the animal, which moves on all fours with the proximal joints always remaining in some degree of flexion. The weakness of the influence of the negative supporting reaction in spastic patients is a great difficulty in walking.

An interesting phenomenon has been observed under treatment which shows that if we can inhibit the positive supporting reaction then we can obtain a definite decrease of extensor tone at the proximal joints. Thus, if a hand is placed under the foot of the standing leg of a spastic patient, strong pressure of the ball of the foot and the clawing of the toes can be felt. This is so whether the heel touches the ground or not, because even if the heel touches the ground the weight is never on it. If the toes are then strongly dorsiflexed against the resistance and maintained in this position for a few seconds, the pressure of the toes will subside and the weight of the body will shift more towards the heel. At the same time the patient's hips and knees will slowly flex and he has an irresistible desire to sit down. If he is asked to remain standing, his legs feel tired and ache, and in the end he will collapse in flexion.

THE CROSSED EXTENSION REFLEX

This reflex was described by Magnus (1926) as follows:

> 'In the standing animal the weight of the hind part of the body is carried by both hind-limbs and the weight of the fore part of the body by both fore-limbs. A painful stimulus applied to one limb evokes the ipsilateral flexion reflex by which the stimulated foot is removed from the neighbourhood of the stimulus. The crossed limb, therefore, has to carry the weight of the fore or hind part of the body alone. This is made possible by the increased supporting reaction as described above, but is aided by the crossed extension reflex, which causes increased tone in the extensor muscles.'

The crossed extension reflex as described by Sherrington (1939) is a spinal reflex following a painful stimulus to one limb and evoking a protective flexion reflex of that limb. Though the spinal animal cannot stand because of the absence of static reflexes, we find already at the spinal level a reflex-coordination, such as the crossed extension reflex, which when combined with the positive supporting reaction enables the animal to stand on one leg, lifting the other. In this way, by the modifying effect of higher activity the lower patterns of coordination are employed in a changed form for movements of higher integration—in this instance for walking.

The crossed extension reflex and its effect on the patient

The reflex increase of extensor tone in the standing leg on lifting the contralateral leg off the ground can be most clearly seen in hemiplegic patients, or in quadruplegic patients in whom the distribution of spasticity is that of a double-hemiplegia, with usually one side considerably less affected than the other, i.e.

with fairly normal tonus. In diplegic patients with pronounced scissor posture and gait the influence of the crossed extension reflex (like that of the negative supporting reaction) cannot be recognized so easily, since these patients are unable to lift either leg to any extent in walking. Both legs are used for weight-bearing most of the time, and the marked extensor spasticity of both legs cannot be inhibited to a sufficient degree to ensure flexion of the moving leg. In such patients if one leg is flexed passively, and the resistance of the extensors is overcome in this way, the standing leg will also flex, and there is a complete absence of the crossed extension reflex. Such patients do not lift their legs off the ground in walking. The 'moving' leg remains semiflexed at hip and knee, but at the same time shows constant exaggerated extensor tone. A slight increase of extensor tone occurs in the standing leg during the short moment when the contralateral one is lifted and moved forward. The patient then rises higher on his toes and somewhat extends his hips by throwing his trunk backwards in order to bring the moving leg forward with a minimum of flexion at hips and knee. This slight extension may be due to the influence of the crossed extension reflex.

Its influence on the hemiplegic patient can be clearly observed during certain stages of treatment. The patient can be taught to stand with the whole weight of the body on the affected leg, the muscles of the leg showing fairly normal tone, i.e. no exaggerated extensor activity. The knee is then mobile and can be actively and passively flexed in spite of weight-bearing; the foot is well dorsiflexed, the heel firmly on the ground and the body-weight over the middle of the foot. This state remains as long as the foot of the sound leg touches the ground. However, at the first attempt at lifting this foot off the ground by bending the sound leg, a strong extensor spasm occurs in the affected leg, owing to the crossed extension reflex. The patient immediately loses his balance because he pushes against the ground with the ball of his foot (positive supporting reaction, reinforcing the extensor spasm); he claws his toes, hyperextends the knee, and only protects himself from falling backwards by flexing the trunk at the hips and bringing the sound leg, together with the whole of the sound side, forward in a step, leaving the affected leg, hip and shoulder behind. This reflex action is very strong and persistent and difficult to stop in treatment. Its strength is due to the augmentation of the crossed extension reflex by the positive supporting reaction. It accounts for the well-known hyperextension of the knee in the hemiplegic's gait, and for his tendency to leave the affected side slightly behind the other in walking.

General static reactions can be demonstrated most easily in the decerebrate animal. They involve more than one segment of the body or the whole body.

General static reactions can be induced by changing either the position of the head relative to the body, or by changing the position of head and body as a whole in space. As a result of the combined reflexes of the labyrinths and the proprioceptors of the muscles of the neck, changes in the distribution of tone throughout the body musculature occur. The most striking reactions occur in the extensors of the limbs and in the neck muscles. As it is possible to impress upon the body different adapted attitudes by changing only the position of the head, Magnus (1926) called these reflexes 'attitudinal reflexes'.

They can be divided into two groups:

1   *Tonic neck reflexes*, evoked by a change in the position of the head in relation to the body, by which the neck receptors are stimulated.

2   *Tonic labyrinthine reflexes*, evoked by a change of orientation of the head in space, which brings the labyrinths into play.

The changes in degree and distribution of tone produced by these reflexes are sustained and last as long as the position of the head remains unchanged.

TONIC NECK REFLEXES

Asymmetrical tonic neck reflexes

They are stimulated by rotation of the head and cause extension

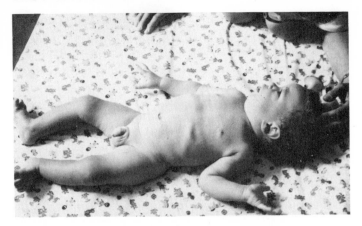

Fig 5.1a

of the limbs towards which the head is rotated (jaw limbs), and decrease of extensor tone with increase of flexion of the limbs towards which the occiput is rotated (skull limbs). (Figs 5.1a and 5.1b.)

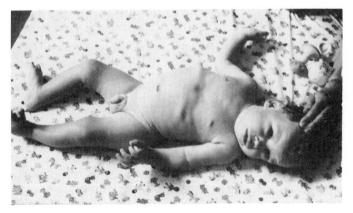

Fig 5.1b

Asymmetrical tonic neck reflexes and their effect on the patient

In many of our spastic patients we find changes of tone throughout the body musculature on rotation of the head to one side. These changes follow the same law as those observed by Magnus in the decerebrate animal. Extensor tone increases in the jaw limbs and decreases in the skull limbs, with a relative increase of flexor tone in the latter. Usually the arms show the reaction more strongly and clearly than the legs. In some cases the reaction is confined to the arms only.

The strength of the reaction varies in individual cases. In the severe case we may see an immediate response on rotating the head, the jaw limbs extending rigidly and the skull limbs flexing. In a less severe case there may be a delay of a few seconds while the head is being rotated, and then the reaction sets in slowly and is less strong. It may, however, occur immediately and strongly if the patient is excited. Walshe (1923) found the reaction to be more pronounced if the patient turned his head actively, and more so if the rotation was carried out with force against resistance.

In many cases, usually in those with slight spasticity whose arms are little affected, the reaction proper cannot be obtained and, although changes of tone may occur, they are not marked enough to result in a visible movement. The testing of the resistance to passive flexion or extension of the limb will, however, reveal these changes of tone. If the arm had flexor spasticity before, it will show decreased resistance to extension on becoming the 'jaw arm' by rotation of the head, and the 'jaw leg', being spastic in extension, will show increased resistance to passive flexion. The skull arm will show increased resistance to extension, the skull leg less resistance to flexion.

In some cases of long standing which show permanent flexor contracture of the elbows, the reaction cannot be elicited, extension of the jaw arm being impossible owing to the contracture, and further flexion of the skull arm impossible as the arm is already maximally flexed.

In our experience asymmetrical tonic neck reflexes are strongest in the supine position or when sitting with the head thrown backwards, while they seem weakest when the patient is lying prone or sitting with the head ventroflexed. The asymmetrical tonic neck reflexes seem to be most active in positions which favour extensor spasticity, and weakest in those favourable for flexor activity. Extensor activity appears to increase the strength of the asymmetrical tonic neck reflexes. This is a point to which further reference will be made when describing the tonic labyrinthine reflexes.

Asymmetrical tonic neck reflexes are usually more easily obtained on turning the head to a particular side. In most of our patients we found the reaction to be more pronounced on rotating the head to the right. Gesell (1941) found that normal babies up to 3 months usually prefer to turn the head more to one side, usually the right.

Release of asymmetrical tonic neck reflexes has a severe effect on the patient's motor behaviour. If the reflexes are strong and occur easily, they dominate it. For instance, the patient can only extend an arm by turning the head to that side, or flex the arm by turning it to the other side. Though he may be able to sit unsupported for a second or two, as long as his head is in midline, the slightest excitation, such as noise, or trying to move or to speak, will produce a spasm in the nature of a tonic neck reflex. Then sudden rotation of the head to one side will occur, and result in a stiffening of that side of the body and the patient will lose his balance.

The patient is usually unable to hold his head in the midline, but will keep it turned to the preferred side. Some patients cannot turn the head to the opposite side, or if they succeed in doing so, it will soon turn back irresistibly to the initial position. In such patients we have observed that they can focus objects easily if they are placed towards the preferred side of rotation, but that moving the eyes towards the midline, or even more to the opposite side when trying to follow a moving object is difficult or impossible. Gesell and Amatruda (1949) have found that normal babies, when still under the influence of the asymmetrical tonic neck reflexes, are equally unable to follow an object if it is moved away from the side of their tonic neck reflex attitude.

The effect of the asymmetrical tonic neck reflex on the arms is most pronounced in the supine position, though similar difficulties of movement of arms and hands can be observed in sitting. The arms remain fixed in the lateral position at the side of the patient's body; the jaw arm is extended, inwards rotated and somewhat adducted, while the skull arm is flexed, retracted at the shoulder and abducted. The patient cannot bring his arms forward to approximate his hands in the midline, and therefore he is unable to hold an object in both hands. He cannot grasp an object held in front of him while looking at it, nor can he bring the object to his mouth. Many children are unable to suck their thumb or fingers because of the extension of the arm on the side to which the face is turned.

Quadruplegic patients with strong asymmetrical tonic neck reflexes, especially if these are more pronounced to one side, are in great danger of developing a scoliosis of the spine if they are made to sit and to use their hands. The sitting balance is very unstable because the distribution of postural tone of one side of the body is totally different from that of the other. The patient tends to fall towards the jaw side, or backwards owing to the added retraction of the head combined with extensor spasticity of the trunk.

The patient usually finds out for himself that sitting is easier if he flexes his head. This counteracts the extensor spasticity of the neck and trunk (*see* tonic labyrinthine reflexes, pp. 44–45) and with it, as mentioned above, weakens the influence of the asymmetrical tonic neck reflexes on the arms and hands. He may be able to keep his sitting balance, but only as long as his head and spine are flexed.

The influence of the asymmetrical tonic neck reflexes on the skull leg may in a very severe case produce, in time, subluxation or dislocation of the hip joint more often of the left than the right hip. We have seen a few cases in which the combination of flexion, inward rotation and adduction of the skull leg with a scoliosis of the spine may have been responsible for this deformity.

The effect of the asymmetrical tonic neck reflex on the legs is usually less strong than that on the arms of the patient. However, we find that some diplegic children have one 'extensor' leg on which they can stand firmly, but which is too stiff to move and make steps easily, (the jaw leg) while the other (the skull leg) can flex and move and make steps forward but does not take the child's weight properly.

Some athetoid children can extend one leg, take weight on it fairly easily while the other, usually the right, makes constant movements of alternate flexion and extension. These movements may be stopped and the child enabled to stand and later on to walk if he turns his face towards the side of the moving leg.

There is a great danger of developing a scoliosis of the spine in children who can only use one hand and predominantly look to that side, and in whom asymmetrical tonic neck reflexes are obligatory. As mentioned above, it is impossible for such a child to move his arms forward so that he can use both hands in midline and look at the object he handles. However, he may be able to employ his tonic neck reflex patterns in order to use one hand, usually the left, for grasping objects and moving them. When reaching out for an object, he may turn his face to one side and bring his extended jaw-arm forward. With his eyes, he can control this part of the movement, which is accompanied by the shoulder of the jaw-arm protracting and that of the skull-arm retracting with flexion of the elbow. The hand of the extended arm, however, is useless for grasping the object. It is either fisted with the wrist extended, or the fingers are open, but with the wrist fully flexed. If the patient intends to grasp the object, he has to turn his face away from it. This gives him the reduction of extensor spasticity and a relative increase of flexor tone, which enables him to pick up the object and to hold it.

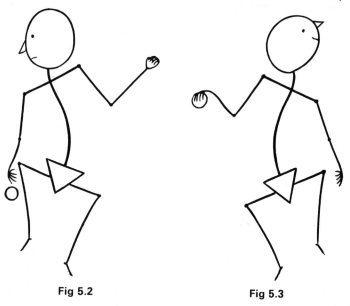

Fig 5.2   **Fig 5.3**

However, he cannot control this part of the movement with his
eyes, since his head is turned away (Figs 5.2 and 5.3).

Though some of the patients use the pattern described above
in reaching out for an object with the jaw arm and then, for
grasping purposes, making it the skull arm by turning the head
away to the opposite side, most of them keep the head turned to
the same side, usually to the right, i.e. away from the grasping
and moving hand. The patient can thus never look at the
object, even when reaching out for it. The most severe scoliosis
of the spine is found among those patients who keep the head
fixed to one and the same side.

The difficulty of grasping an object with the jaw arm is
explained by Fulton (1951) who describes thalamic patterns in
semidecorticated monkeys. When lying in the lateral position
the monkey's undermost extremities were rigidly extended and
did not show a grasp reflex, while the uppermost extremities

were strongly flexed and invariably showed the grasp reflex. In this connection it seems an interesting point that the majority of patients with cerebral palsy appear to be left-handed. The fact that in most of these cases asymmetrical tonic neck reflexes are more pronounced on turning the head to the right than to the left may be responsible for their 'left-handedness'.

While it is most difficult for patients with asymmetrical tonic neck reflexes to learn to sit and use their hands, it is quite impossible for them to learn to stand and walk. Most patients with marked asymmetrical tonic neck reflex patterns will not even attempt to do so. The changes of the distribution of tone on rotation of the head lead to sudden upsets of the equilibrium, with collapse on the side of the skull limbs. This may occur even in the lighter cases which show less marked asymmetrical tonic neck reflex patterns in lying supine and sitting, but in whom the influence of asymmetrical tonic neck reflexes becomes more marked under the stress, both physical and emotional, of trying to keep their balance in standing and walking.

A case report on a child who showed intermittently the effect of asymmetrical tonic neck reflexes and who had learned to stand for a second or two and make a few steps with support will illustrate these points:

E.P. aged 10 years, a spastic child with athetoid movements, strong asymmetrical tonic neck reflexes in all positions, with preference to the right side. She has learned to control them to some extent in sitting by keeping her head well flexed. In this position she can hold her head in midline and can use both her hands. If the child is put on her feet she reacts almost instantly with a strong extensor spasm in both legs, trunk and neck. This is probably due to the influence of the positive supporting reaction. The whole body extends rigidly, she stands on her toes, the legs are adducted and inward rotated, the head thrown backwards. She would fall backwards if not held. After a second of this extensor spasm she turns her head to the right; the hip and knee of the left leg flexes simultaneously and the child's trunk bends over to the right, the left arm flexion and raised in abduction. If not held she would collapse to the right side and fall to the ground. The patient can be made to

stand, however, but only with the head in ventroflexion. Then she
has to be helped to keep her hips and knees extended, since
otherwise she would not have sufficient extensor tone for standing.
She can even make a few fairly normal steps, but she will suddenly
extend rigidly and turn her head to the right with the result
described above (Fig. 5.4).

Fig 5.4

Symmetrical tonic neck reflexes

These reactions are evoked by the dorsiflexion or ventroflexion
of the head. The stimulus arises in the proprioceptors of the
muscles of the neck.

Dorsiflexion of the head leads to increase of extensor tone in
the fore-limbs, and a decrease of extensor tone with a relative
increase of flexor tone in the hind-limbs of an animal.
Ventroflexion of the head has the opposite effect on the limbs;

on lowering the head of the animal the fore-limbs flex and the hind-limbs extend.

The functional significance of these reactions will be well appreciated when watching a cat drinking milk from a saucer. If the cat lowers the head to drink, the front legs will be seen to flex and the hind-limbs to extend. If some food is held above the cat's head, the animal will lift its head, extend the fore-limbs and sit down on its hind-legs. This is the most favourable position for jumping towards its prey (Figs 5.5 and 5.6).

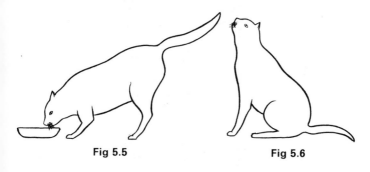

Fig 5.5   **Fig 5.6**

Symmetrical tonic neck reflexes and their effect on the patient

Symmetrical tonic neck reflexes and their effect on patients have not been studied as extensively as the effects of asymmetrical tonic neck reflexes.

Usually patients who show the influence of symmetrical tonic neck reflexes show that of asymmetrical ones as well, but occasionally only the symmetrical reflexes are found to be active.

They can be tested in the following way:

Patients with pronounced flexor spasticity will be unable, when placed on their knees, to put their hands flat on the ground and to support their weight on their arms. The head is then flexed, the shoulder girdle protracted, the arms

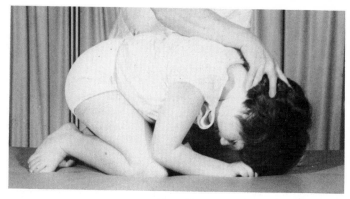

Fig 5.7

adducted, flexed at the elbows, the hands tightly clenched and the ankles dorsiflexed (Fig 5.7).

If the head is now passively lifted, supported under the chin, or the shoulder girdle pulled backwards, most patients will, after some delay, extend their arms and place the hands to the ground. As long as the head is supported in dorsiflexion the arms will remain extended, but the moment the head is released and allowed to flex again, the arms will flex as well and the patient will draw his hands up to the chest and fall on his face if not supported (Figs 5.8 and 5.9).

The effect of the symmetrical tonic neck reflexes in producing changes of the distribution of tone in the arms of patients can thus be clearly observed. The effect of such tonus changes on the legs can also be noted in many patients, though they are often less marked.

They can be tested as follows:

The patient, when placed in the prone position, usually shows ventroflexion of the head, and flexion and adduction of the arms. The legs are extended and offer resistance to passive flexion at hips and knees, so that it is difficult to place him on

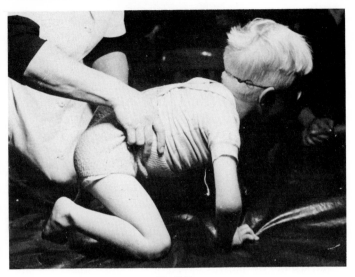

Fig 5.8

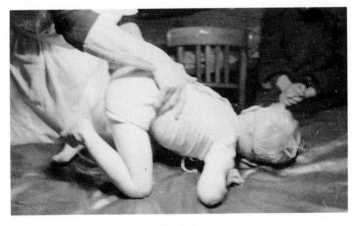

Fig 5.9

Fig 5.10

his knees (Fig 5.10). This is due to the influence of the symmetrical tonic neck reflexes, as can be proved by lifting the head of the patient passively, supported under the chin. The arms then extend, and hips and knees flex automatically (Fig 5.11) and even dorsiflexion of the feet may occur

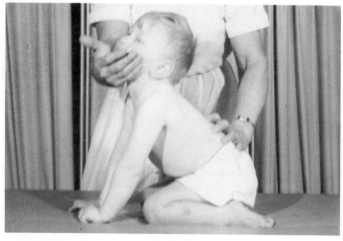

Fig 5.11

spontaneously, whereas before passive dorsiflexion was
strongly resisted. In this way the patient can be made to sit on
his heels easily (Fig 5.11). However, from this position, as
long as the head is raised, it may be impossible to move the
patient's trunk forward, and bring his weight on to hands and
knees and his seat off his feet. He cannot extend his hips and
knees; they remain flexed when the trunk is moved forward so
that the feet are raised from the ground (Fig 5.12).

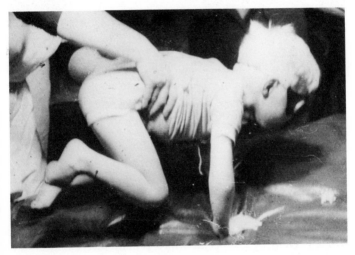

Fig 5.12

If, however, the feet are held passively in plantiflexion on
the ground while the patient's trunk is moved forward, thus
extending the knees, an extensor spasm occurs. The head and
arms flex and the patient's body shoots forward due to the
sudden extension of hips and knees. If care is not taken he
may fall on his face (Fig 5.13).

The same observation can be made in patients who show a
severe degree of extensor spasticity of the legs so that they offer

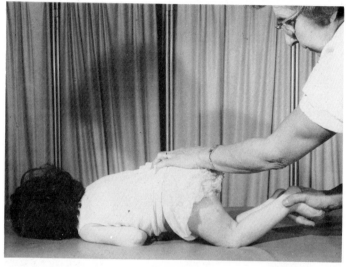

Fig 5.13

strong resistance to passive flexion if one tries to place them on
their knees. After one has overcome the resistance of the
extensor muscles, they may be able to maintain the heel-sitting
posture as long as the head is raised. In these cases it is easy to
move the trunk forward, i.e. to extend hips and knees. They do
not show a flexor spasm but, after a few degrees of extension, a
strong extensor spasm occurs which is more severe than in the
former case. The patient's trunk shoots forward as described
above, the arms and head in flexion.

These observations show that not only the distribution of
tone in the arms, but also in the legs varies with the change of
the position of the head. Raising the head produces an increase
of flexor tone in the legs. Ventroflexion of the head has the
opposite effect. These changes of tone are relative and not
absolute. Thus, in a patient with marked extensor spasticity of a
limb the influence of a tonic reflex in the direction of an increase
of flexor activity may result only in a reduction of the degree of
extensor spasticity, and not necessarily in spontaneous flexion.

Patients who strongly show the effect of the above reactions are usually unable to keep their balance in the quadrupedal position or support their body-weight on hands and knees. They cannot crawl in a normal manner. They may be able to progress in the heel-sitting posture by placing the extended arms forward with the head raised, and dragging the flexed legs forward towards the arms. They remain sitting on their heels and do not extend hips and knees. This will in time result in flexor contractures of hips and knees.

Other, less severely affected patients, may be able to support their body-weight on hands and knees, but only so long as the head is well raised. If the head is flexed, the elbows bend and the patient collapses. Such patients may be able to crawl, but usually not with normal coordination (Figs 5.14 and 5.15). In

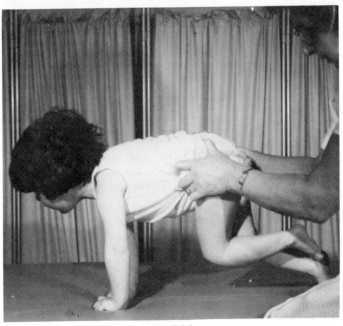

Fig 5.14

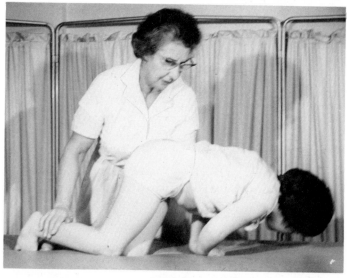

Fig 5.15

this latter type of patient, who shows strong extension of the arms while the head is raised, the influence of the asymmetrical tonic neck reflexes is often combined with that of the symmetrical ones. Such a patient in kneeling supports himself well on his hands and knees, but if the face is turned to one side, he may collapse on the skull arm, that arm flexing and the shoulder pulling forward and downwards.

It will be seen that the dependence of the distribution of tone in arms and legs on the position of the head can be a serious obstacle to learning to crawl reciprocally. Even in the lighter cases in which the tonic neck reflexes produce only slight changes of tone, these changes interfere with the movements, limit their range and produce abnormal coordination in crawling. In the severe cases, however, these changes of tone are in the nature of sustained and strong tonic spasms, which fix the patient in certain postures and make movements away from them impossible.

TONIC LABYRINTHINE REFLEXES

These reflexes can only be studied separately by excluding the tonic neck reflexes. In his animal experiments Magnus (1926) did this by either cutting the first three cervical posterior roots, thus interrupting the sensory part of the reflex arc for the tonic neck reflexes, or by immobilizing head, neck and trunk in a plaster jacket, thus excluding the possibility of changing the head position in relation to the trunk. Magnus found that:

> 'There is only one position in which the extensor tone becomes maximal: the supine position with snout about 45° above the horizontal plane. The extensor tone diminishes to a relative minimum if the animal is brought into the prone position with snout about 45° below the horizontal plane. The minimum and maximum positions differ, therefore, by 180°. In all other positions in space the extensor tone is intermediate between the two extremes. These reflexes are not evoked by movement but depend upon position. . . . Only such changes in the position of the head are effective as change in its angle in relation to the horizontal plane.'

Tonic labyrinthine reflexes and their effect on the patient

It is most difficult to study tonic labyrinthine reflexes in isolation on patients because of their close interaction with tonic neck—and other—reflexes.

In the individual case the influence of either the tonic neck or tonic labyrinthine reflexes may be predominant and decide the type of the patient's motor-reactions. Magnus (1924) has made similar observations on animals, finding in some of them the tonic neck reflexes and in others the tonic labyrinthine reflexes more dominant. He states the distinguishing factor to be the reaction of the limbs to a movement of the head. If by the movement of the head all four limbs are affected in the same sense, the tonic labyrinthine reflexes dominate. If the head movement produces tonus changes in the limbs, which affect one side of the body differently from the other, or the fore-limbs

differently from the hind-limbs, the tonic neck reflexes dominate. Magnus found that he could test the dominance of one or
the other group of tonic reflexes best when the animal was in the
side lying position.

We have not been able to test our patients in this way and we
cannot say whether the observed tonus changes can in every
case be ascribed to the influence of the tonic labyrinthine
reflexes only.

As mentioned above with regard to the tonic neck reflexes,
the changes of tone brought about by the tonic labyrinthine
reflexes are also relative. A diminution of extensor spasticity due
to the influence of a tonic labyrinthine reflex does not
necessarily mean that the limb will be seen to flex. The limb
may only offer less resistance to passive flexion but, nevertheless, show extensor spasticity though of a lesser degree.

As in Magnus's animal experiments, and as Walshe (1923)
in patients, we found maximal extensor tone with the
patient in the supine position (Fig 5.16). We also noticed that
the same patients who in this position showed severe extensor
spasticity showed marked flexor spasticity in prone lying.

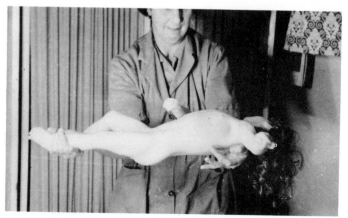

Fig 5.16

Patients who in the supine position showed severe retraction of the neck and rigid extension of the spine and retracted shoulders, showed in the prone position a kyphosis of the dorsal spine (produced by the spastic contraction of the pectoral and abdominal muscles) and adducted and flexed arms. They were unable to raise the head off the support (Fig 5.17).

In a few cases extensor spasticity was so marked in all positions that these patients were able to hold the head up in prone, the spine and legs rigidly extended. Extensor spasticity was weaker in prone than in supine, but still so pronounced that there was considerable resistance to passive flexion of the head. If the head was ventroflexed, however, and held in this position, the patient showed marked increase of flexor tone in the trunk and arms, with a kyphosis of the dorsal spine due to spastic contraction of the flexor muscles of the trunk and shoulders.

Most patients show rigid extension and adduction of the legs in the supine position. However, a number of patients, usually the older ones who have been made to sit and those who walk with scissor gait, show some flexions at hips and knees (cocontraction of flexors and extensors). In these cases it may be

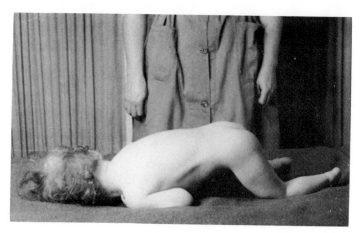

Fig 5.17

impossible to obtain the prone lying position because of a strong increase of the already existing flexor spasm at the hips when turning them over to prone lying from supine.

All patients are most rigid, i.e. show strongest extensor spasticity, in supine, but when made to sit with the head flexed well forward, the back appears weak, extensor spasticity being reduced or absent and flexor spasticity becoming dominant. The increase of flexor tone can be tested by trying to extend the flexed spine passively without allowing the hips to extend. Strong resistance to extension will then be encountered, especially of the lumbar spine, and if one succeeds in extending the spine by force, the hips will extend simultaneously and the patient be unable to sit (Fig 5.18).

While in the supine position the legs may be rigidly extended and adducted at the hips; in sitting a considerable degree of abduction may be possible, abduction being part of the flexor pattern.

On trying to make a patient sit up from supine, one usually

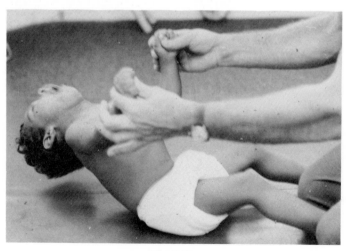

Fig 5.18

experiences initial resistance by the extensors of the hips. When the patient is lifted about half-way up to a sitting position, the resistance will suddenly cease, as the head assumes a position in space more favourable for flexor activity. At this moment the spine, which has been in extension before, will become flexed, and the shoulders which were retracted will become protracted. This tendency to flexion increases until the patient arrives in the sitting posture, and will cause the head to fall forward with a further increase of flexion of the spine (Fig. 5.19). At this point some patients are in danger of falling forward, especially those who show strong flexor spasticity at the hips as well as extensor spasticity, while in others the hips remain in semiextension while the whole spine is strongly flexed. However, if the patient's head is raised passively, or if he throws his head backwards, the picture changes again almost instantly. Flexor activity gives way again to extensor spasticity and the patient will be in danger of falling backwards.

Though these changes of tone are chiefly caused by the

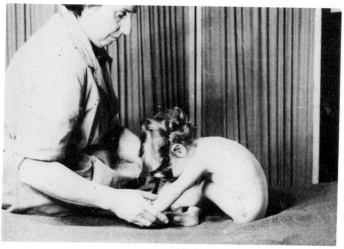

Fig 5.19

influence of the tonic labyrinthine reflexes, these reflexes may not be entirely responsible for the reactions, as the tonic neck reflexes are usually active as well and may contribute their effect on the patient's motor reactions.

The patient's ability to move is severely restricted by these tonus changes. In the supine position he will be unable to lift his head. The activity of the flexor muscles of the hips and of the abdominal muscles is inhibited by the excessive tone in the extensors of hips and trunk. He is therefore unable to sit up by himself, and this difficulty is increased by the retraction of the arms at the shoulders, which prevents him from bringing his arms forward to pull himself up (Fig 5.20).

The strong extensor spasticity in the supine position prevents the patient from turning to his side, because flexion and rotation forward of the shoulder and hip of one side is impossible. For instance, if attempting to turn to the left side, he is unable to bring the right arm forward and across the body, or flex the right leg and move it across the other leg. His difficulties are intensified if asymmetrical tonic neck reflexes are present.

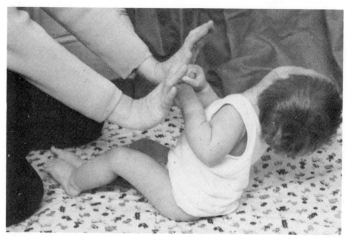

Fig 5.20

Although by rotating the face to one side, as a first stage of turning on to the side, the skull arm may flex, the shoulder and trunk of the skull side will retract and prevent the shoulder and thorax from following the head.

On trying to turn from the side lying position to prone, the face is first turned towards the support. This, owing to the action of the tonic labyrinthine reflexes, leads to flexor spasticity in the trunk, arms and hips, which prevents the patient from turning on his stomach. He is unable to extend the hips and knees and to raise the shoulder girdle sufficiently to bring his arms forward from their position under his chest.

In prone lying most patients are unable to raise the head and to extend the spine, or to support themselves on their forearms, or to support themselves on their hands with extended arms (Fig 5.21).

Exceptions to this are those few cases which show such degree of extensor spasticity that even in the prone position extensor activity, though reduced, is still dominant. These patients can raise their head and extend the spine, but their difficulty is to

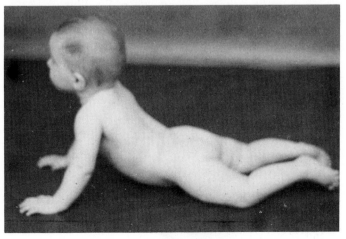

Fig 5.21

ventroflex the head. If this is done passively, they show an excess
of flexor tone and cannot support themselves on their arms and
hands.

ASSOCIATED REACTIONS

Another type of postural reflex which becomes released in
spastic patients is the 'associated reactions'. They have been
studied by Walshe (1923) who found that tonic and sustained
contractions of the muscles of the sound limbs, such as for
instance forceful grasping of an object with the sound hand,
produced an increase of tone in the spastic muscles of the
affected side in a hemiplegic patient. These increases of tone led
either to a movement, such as flexion of the affected arms, or to
a palpable increase of flexor tone. The movements produced in
this way were due to an increase of tone and not movements in
the strict sense. For this reason Walshe suggested calling them
'associated reactions' rather than 'associated movements' as
they were named before. He defined them as 'tonic reflexes
arising in the limb muscles and acting on the limb muscles' in
contrast to 'tonic reflexes acting from the head on the limbs'. To
quote Walshe:

> '. . . all voluntary movements are accompanied by an appropriate
> postural adjustment of the rest of the skeletal musculature, and in
> forceful movements this adjustment or adaptation is necessarily
> bilateral and widespread. Although carried out under voluntary
> control, postural adaptation is a function of reflex mechanisms,
> situated in the brainstem, which are not put out of action by the
> lesion which produced hemiplegia and abolishes voluntary control
> of the musculature on the affected side of the body. In these
> circumstances, we should still expect postural reactions to occur
> when forceful, voluntary motor activities are carried out by the
> musculature of the sound half of the body. Now, however, deprived
> of cortical control, they would occur in exaggerated intensity and
> deprived of that fineness and adaptation which that control ensures.'

In order to elicit associated reactions on the paralyzed side Walshe chose the stimulus of a tonic voluntary contraction of the muscles of the sound limb. He found, however, that other stimuli such as clenching of the jaw, yawning and stiffening the neck muscles produced associated reactions. Furthermore, voluntary contractions of the muscles of one paralyzed limb, as for instance an attempt at a movement, produced associated reactions in the other spastic limb.

Walshe continues by writing about 'conditions governing the occurence of associated reactions'. He says:

'In none of the flaccid cases examined was any sign of associated reactions in arm or leg detected. In the spastic cases, on the other hand, a more or less well developed reaction of forceful voluntary activity of the normal limbs was constant. In two cases, indeed, no excursion of the paralyzed arm occured, but palpation revealed a distinct access of spasticity during the performance of the voluntary movements. We may say, therefore, that some degree of hypertonus in a case of hemiplegia is an essential preliminary to the development of associated reaction. The higher the degree of spasticity present, the more forceful and the longer lasting will be the associated reaction. . . .

'In short, the adequate stimulus for an associated reaction in the muscles of the hemiplegic part of the body is strong, voluntary muscular contraction. . . . Passive movements of the limbs have not been found to be effective in producing associated reactions. . . .

'The duration of an associated reaction is roughly that of the voluntary movement or contraction evoking it, but there is in some instances a prolonged aftercontraction or tonic prolongation of spasm, which may last for several seconds. In one case this was still of undiminished intensity after the elapse of 48 seconds. While the reaction persists, the limb maintains the new attitude more or less steadily. . . . In general, it may be stated that the more spastic the limb, the longer the latency and aftercontraction.

'It is a fact that antagonistic muscle groups, extensor and flexor, are to be observed in simultaneous contraction in such an associated reaction as we have described.'

Associated reactions and their effect on the patient

Though associated reactions have been studied mainly on hemiplegic patients, they can be observed equally well in diplegic cases in the legs. Here they occur when the patient tries hard to perform a movement such as grasping an object or making a step. For this the diplegic patient and the quad-ruplegic spastic patient always uses force and effort, as he is always struggling to overcome the resistance of the spastic muscles. As Walshe has observed, we found in cases with severe spasticity that the movements produced by associated reactions were small, and sometimes only a further stiffening of the muscles could be observed which found expression in an intensification of the initial posture of either flexion or exten-sion. In the less severely spastic patients the tonic changes produced by associated reactions ensued in movements of a fairly wide range which, since they affected all limbs, sometimes resembled involuntary movements.

> 'Associated reactions are tonic postural reactions—that is reflex variations in muscle tone rather than movements in the strict physiological sense' (Walshe, 1923).

In contrast to 'associated reactions', 'associated movements', also called 'synkinisis', are normally coordinated movements in the absence of spasticity. They occur as a result of reinforcement to movements initiated and performed with effort and with the difficulties of learning a new skill. They produce widespread motor responses to stimuli—usually on the opposite side of the body—when inhibition of unwanted parts of the movements has not made detailed discriminate movements possible. They can be seen in normal children's early motor development. Fog (1963) says:

> 'In the mature and uninjured brain, no associated movements occur when daily life activities or well trained motor performances are executed. If, however, the brain is injured—and especially if the damage has taken place early in life—or if an adult has to learn an unaccustomed and complicated hand-performance, associated movements can be observed.'

The detrimental effect of associated reactions does not seem to have been sufficiently recognized in treatment. The increase of spasticity in some parts of the body produced by the forceful activity of other parts is one factor which is responsible for many deformities. For instance, it is a well known fact that the forceful flexion of the affected leg in the hemiplegic patient produces associated reactions in the affected arm by an increase of flexion of elbow, wrist and fingers. If a hemiplegic patient, lying supine, is asked to flex his spastic leg against the resistance of the hypertonic extensors, the effort to do so will always lead to an increase of flexor tone in the affected arm. The same patient may be able to stand with the arm in a fairly extended position, but if he lifts the affected leg to make a step, the arm and hand will contract in flexion. During the first few steps this flexion of the arm will increase to a maximum, which varies with the individual patient. The arm and hand will then remain in the new posture of increased flexion. As patients are walking about a good deal during the day, no decrease of flexor spasticity of arm and hand and recovery of the use of the fingers can be expected so long as associated reactions are active.

Increase of flexor spasticity in the muscles of the affected arm and hand is also produced by every activity of the sound hand, such as writing, dressing and other purposive movements. This presents a problem even in patients with slighter degrees of spasticity who are able to use their affected hand to some extent. These patients rarely use the affected arm and hand spontaneously; they have to think about it, and by preference use the sound hand only. This produces increase of flexor tone in the affected arm and serves to maintain spasticity and thus counteracts the recovery of hand and fingers.

It is of interest to observe the detrimental effect of associated reactions in babies with hemiplegia. Until about 8 months of age, diagnosis is difficult because spasticity in arm and leg is very slight. The affected hand still opens, but is fisted more often and for longer periods of time than the sound one. He does not use the sound hand yet for any tasks and he has no

difficulties with balance yet. However, when such a baby starts
to use his sound hand, he naturally looks to that side and turns
his face away from the affected hand which he cannot use. The
voluntary effort of using the sound hand with the face turned
away from the affected one produces associated reactions with
increased flexion and pronation of the affected arm and hand
(Figs 5.22; 5.23). This represents the interaction of the asymmetrical tonic neck reflex with associated reactions. The
affected leg does not show spasticity with plantiflexion of the
foot until the child begins to stand and walk. Difficulty in
putting the heel down becomes most pronounced at a later
stage when the child starts to run about and at the same time
the arm and hand will become more spastic in flexion.

The influence of associated reactions produced by forceful
contractions of the spastic arm on the affected leg has been
observed during treatment, when trying to obtain voluntary
extension of the elbow and hand.

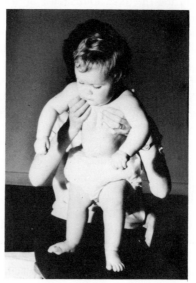

Fig 5.22

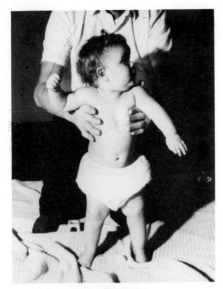

Fig 5.23

Example: The patient was an elderly man who suffered from a left-sided residual hemiplegia after a vascular lesion. His leg was fairly normal and showed only very slight spasticity. His coordination in walking was normal. He could place his heel to the ground first, heel-toe walk, and he flexed his knee sufficiently to clear the ground with his foot without circumduction at the hip. His arm, however, was in considerable flexor spasm, and he could not extend the elbow, elevate the arm, extend his wrist or open his fingers.

Treatment was concentrated on obtaining extensor activity. Elevation of the arm was practised and active and resisted movements of extension of the elbow were given, while wrist and fingers were passively extended and held in this position.

After a few weeks the patient could actively elevate the arm when lying supine, and raise it above the horizontal plane in sitting and standing. He could extend the elbow with the arm flexed forward at the shoulder, but after such extension the arm exhibited strong resistance to passive flexion of the elbow. This resistance to passive flexion and an inability to flex the elbow actively, was seen not only when the arm was flexed forward at the shoulder, but also after elevation in supine. There was still considerable flexor spasticity of wrist and fingers, though it was slightly decreased, and the patient could extend the wrist actively, but his fingers then showed increased flexion.

After three months of treatment the patient complained that his foot turned inwards, and that the knee felt stiff. He was then walking with slight circumduction, hardly flexing the knee, turning his foot inwards with the weight on its lateral border, and placing the ball of the foot down first, the heel afterwards. His balance had become more unstable and he showed strong flexor spasticity of the arm in walking. On examination of the leg, it was found that there was considerable resistance to passive flexion of hip and knee and to adduction of the hip when the leg was flexed. Resistance to dorsiflexion of the foot had also increased though full dorsiflexion was still possible.

This example shows a mistake in treatment and the danger of using resisted exercises in spastic conditions. Deterioration of the condition of the leg, i.e. increase of extensor spasticity, occurred as a result of the repeated exercises of the extensors of the elbow.

As already mentioned, undesirable reinforcement of tone in spastic muscles due to associated reactions occur not only in hemiplegic but also in diplegic and quadruplegic patients. If, for instance, a diplegic patient is made to use one hand in sitting—a position favouring flexor spasticity—the effort may produce an increase of flexor spasticity in the opposite arm, neck, trunk and hips. Such activities may in time become a contributory factor in producing flexor deformities.

Increase of extensor spasticity with adduction and inward rotation of the legs can be seen in diplegic babies and very young children whose legs have little spasticity and good abduction in flexion before they pull themselves along the floor with their arms. The effort in using their less affected upper extremities produces associated increase of extensor spasticity in the legs. This may result in contractures of the adductors and inward rotators of the hips and of the extensors of knees and ankles.

COMBINED ACTION OF ATTITUDINAL REFLEXES

The above interpretation of the effect of released tonic reflexes on the motor behaviour of patients has been arrived at by observation and deduction. There are great difficulties in determining which reflex plays a dominant role at any particular moment in producing a certain reaction. The deductions, therefore, ascribing a specific reaction of the patient to the influence of one or the other reflex, may not be correct in all instances. Only rarely is an observed reaction the result of the influence of one single reflex. More often the reaction is due to the interaction of a number of reflexes, some reinforcing, some neutralizing and some inhibiting each other. The examples which have been chosen are those showing most clearly the action of one or the other reflex influence dominant at the time, resulting in typical and predictable changes of tone throughout the body musculature.

The combined action of tonic reflexes has already been mentioned in some of the examples demonstrating the domin-ance of individual tonic reflexes. In the description of the crossed extension reflex, it was shown that the positive supporting reaction reinforces the extensor spasticity of the standing leg in the hemiplegic patient when he lifts the sound leg off the ground. The combination of symmetrical and asymmetrical tonic neck reflexes has been described in patients who can support their weight on their extended arms in kneeling as long as the head is dorsiflexed. On turning the face to the side, however, they flex the skull arm and extend the face arm rigidly.

The interaction of tonic labyrinthine and tonic neck reflexes can be observed in many instances. For example, a hemiplegic patient lying in the supine position will show strong resistance to passive flexion of the affected leg when the face is turned towards the affected side. If the face is turned to the opposite side, resistance to flexion will be decreased. Still further decrease of extensor tone in the affected leg may be obtained by placing the patient in the prone position with the face turned towards the sound side, and complete inhibition of extensor spasticity of the affected leg may occur when the patient is made to kneel. In this position a flexor spasm may occur in the leg, and the foot, which formerly resisted passive dorsiflexion, may then flex spontaneously at the ankle and offer resistance to passive plantiflexion.

Another example can be seen in the different reaction of the jaw arm of a diplegic patient according to whether he is in the supine or sitting position. Extension of the arm to which the face is turned is maximal in supine, when tonic labyrinthine reflexes augment the extensor tone produced by the asymmetrical tonic neck reflexes. The same patient, however, in the sitting position with the head ventroflexed, may not show extension of the arm when the face is turned towards that side, or if he does, resistance to passive flexion of the elbow will be considerably less than it was in the supine position.

Walshe (1923) has studied the modifying effect of the tonic neck and tonic labyrinthine reflexes on the degree and distribution of tone in the arm of hemiplegic patients. He found different forms of associated reactions in the hemiplegic arm following a change of position of the head in relation to the horizontal plane, i.e. on placing the patient supine, prone or in the lateral positions. He ascribed the changes of tone resulting from these changes in position to the tonic labyrinthine reflex influence. He also obtained changes in the form of associated reactions on altering the position of the head in relation to the trunk, and ascribed them to the influence of tonic neck reflexes. The various combinations of these reflexes, sometimes reinforcing and sometimes antagonizing each other, were tested by Walshe on a case of thrombotic right hemiplegia. His examples show the varying reactions of the patient's affected arm in five different positions of his head and body.

The great difficulty in interpreting the combined action of reflexes may be illustrated in the following examples of reactions of patients:

1 Diplegic patients when standing may be able to keep their heels on the ground as long as the head is ventroflexed. When looking up, however, or if the head is raised passively, they stand on their toes. This could be explained by the influence of tonic labyrinthine reflexes, increasing extensor tone in the legs during dorsiflexion of the head, but according to the influence of the symmetrical tonic neck reflexes, one would expect a flexion of the legs at this moment. The same patient in four-foot kneeling may show the influence of the symmetrical tonic neck reflexes during dorsiflexion of the head, i.e. flexion of the legs and extension of the arms.

2 We observed strong asymmetrical tonic neck reflexes in a young diplegic patient in the supine position. On turning the face to one side, the jaw arm and leg extended on that side, while the skull limbs flexed. When the patient was lying prone, however, the opposite reaction occurred: the jaw limbs flexed strongly on turning the head to that side, while the skull limbs extended. This reversal of the asymmetrical tonic neck reflex pattern in prone lying may be due to its inhibition by the normal, but primitive, creeping pattern. Temple Fay (verbal communication) has found that some children who could not feed themselves because of stiff extension of their 'face-arm', due to asymmetrical tonic neck reflex activity, could do so in a 'quasi-prone' position, such as sitting well bent forward at a table, their head and arms supported on the table.

We have observed many more reactions of this kind, which we are unable to explain, but which must be due to the combined action of certain reflexes.

The interaction of tonic neck and tonic labyrinthine reflexes has been studied by Magnus. His observations on animals may serve as illustrations of the interplay between different types of reflexes. According to Magnus, tonic neck and tonic labyrinthine reflexes, if they are both active, cooperate in such a way that the tone of every muscle depends on the algebraic sum of the influences from the proprioceptors of the neck and from the labyrinths. If, for instance, the extensors of the arm derive increase of tone from the labyrinths and the neck, the combined result will be strongest extensor tone in that arm. If both neck and labyrinths act in the direction of diminution of extensor tone, the result will be minimal extensor tone in that arm. If muscle tone is increased from the labyrinths and decreased from the neck, the result will be a compromise, depending upon the relative strength of these influences. Thus, if the labyrinthine influence predominates, the elbow will be extended, while if the neck reflexes predominate the arm will be flexed. If the reflexes are equal in strength the angle of the elbow will not change at all. Magnus says:

'This cooperation gives rise to very characteristic attitudinal reactions of the decerebrate animal. Place a cat in the prone position upon the table and flex the head ventrally, then the labyrinths come into the minimum position and all four limbs will tend to relax. The neck influences cause relaxation of the fore-limbs and cooperate in the fore-limbs, which show distinct relaxation, whereas the hind-limbs may not change at all, because the influence from neck and labyrinths act in opposite sense. If with the prone position of the animal the head is bent dorsally, the resulting removal of the labyrinths from the minimal position causes extension of all four limbs. The neck reflexes evoke extension of the fore-limbs and relaxation of the hind-limbs. The combined effect is only slight changes in the hind-limbs. Head movements, therefore, in a ventral and dorsal direction have a very strong influence on the fore-limbs, whereas the reaction of the hind-limbs is much weaker.'

Walshe (1923) has described a method of determining the relative predominance of tonic neck and tonic labyrinthine reflexes in hemiplegic patients. He suggests placing the patient in the lateral position, the hemiplegic side down, the sound side uppermost. He found that if the face was turned upwards (away from the hemiplegic side by a rotation of the head), associated extension occurred in the hemiplegic arm only if the labyrinthine reflexes were active. If, however, the arm was flexed, the neck reflexes predominated.

In the previous chapters, tonic, or static, reflexes were discussed and their influence on patients with upper motor neurone lesions were noted when they became released from higher control, that is, when they became hyperactive, exaggerated and dominated the patient's motor behaviour. Their association with hypertonus of varying degrees and distribution was considered, spasticity being seen as a release phenomenon of exaggerated tonic reflex activity coordinated in the patterns of various tonic reflexes interacting with each other. Released tonic reflexes represent what might be called 'abnormal and static postural reflex activity' which interferes with and inhibits normal postural reactions such as the righting and equilibrium reactions, which are normal protective reactions of a stato-kinetic character and form the automatic background of coordination for our more voluntary skilled and 'learned' movements.

Normal postural reflex activity consists of a great number of stato-kinetic postural reactions which interact with and reinforce each other. They combine the automatic movements of adjustment to changes of posture, such as righting and equilibrium reactions, with antigravity action and fixation of proximal parts of the body and limbs to movements performed distally. The balanced interaction of stato-kinetic postural reactions in the normal person makes weightbearing with mobility possible. Postural control is dynamic and involves a great variety of well coordinated movement patterns and tonus changes. Kinnier Wilson (1925), speaking about the tendency to differentiate, rigorously and schematically, movement from posture and kinetic from static muscular contraction, says:

'Speaking generally, *volition* is taken to imply movement, and reflex action posture, yet the inapplicability of the generalization must be plain to the reader. Posture is often maintained *voluntarily* and much reflex action is of a definite kinetic character. Movement is in reality a series of changes of posture, and Sherrington has stated that the distinction between reflexes of posture and reflexes of movement is not clear cut.'

The various postural reactions in the normal person are coordinated in definite patterns which are common to all of us, and subcortically controlled. Although they occur automatically, they are active movements, as active as any voluntary movement. Critchley (1954), when discussing volitional movement, stated that:

'all associated muscular activity becomes regulated, though not at a conscious level, so as to form a harmony of movement, of which the prime movers carry out the deliberate, volitional, conscious part of the act, the other components of the movement taking place at various levels of unawareness . . .'

The motor patterns of normal postural reactions develop in the child gradually during the first few years of life and have been called by Schaltenbrand 'principal motility'. All voluntary and skilled functional activity with its complex and selective patterns of coordination is derived from, and performed on, the background of automatic postural reaction patterns. This means that 'willed' movements are only partly voluntary, as they are based on and supported by automatic movements and tonus changes. The sequential development of early childhood gives us the means of studying the development of coordination, especially that of righting and equilibrium reaction. This knowledge is not only important when treating children, but is equally important for the treatment of any defects of coordination, whether in the child or adult. It is, therefore, essential for the treatment of all patients with upper motor neurone lesions in whom postural reflex activity and postural tone are abnormal and in whom many of the most important automatic motor patterns of normal postural reactions are missing, factors which result in an abnormal performance of voluntary movements (Bobath, 1969).

The normal postural reflex mechanism consists mainly of two types of automatic reactions, the righting and the equilibrium reactions. The former have been studied by Schaltenbrand (1925, 1926, 1927), on a large number of babies and young children. He has described the sequence of their appearance during the growth and maturation of babies and their modification and partial inhibition during childhood.

The gradual development of these righting reactions underlies and explains the sequence of development of the growing child's spontaneous motor abilities at various stages, as described by André-Thomas (1940), Gesell and Amatruda (1949), Illingworth (1960), André-Thomas, Dargassies and Chesni (1952, 1960), McGraw (1963) and others. Equilibrium reactions have been studied and described by Rademaker (1935), Weisz (1938), Zador (1938) and others.

Both types of reactions develop in a definite sequence. However, whereas righting reactions are active from birth onwards, the more highly developed and more complex equilibrium reactions begin to appear around the 7th month, when the righting reactions have become fully established. The righting mechanism becomes part of the equilibrium reactions, though the equilibrium reactions and the child's volitional activities serve to modify the patterns of the righting reactions, some becoming partially inhibited, some disappearing altogether between three and five years of age.

EXPERIMENTAL STUDIES ON ANIMALS

Though decerebrate animals can stand when put on their feet, they are unable to maintain their balance or to right themselves when pushed over. They are solely under the influence of the tonic attitudinal reflexes described above and they lack righting reflexes. Magnus (1926) showed in his experiments on cats and dogs that transection of the neuraxis at a higher level, i.e. not below the most oral part of the midbrain, leads to a complete change in the behaviour of the animal. While transection below this level results in decerebrate rigidity, the higher cut produces a normal distribution of tone and active righting reflexes. Owing to this the animal can now right itself by its own active movements and maintain its balance against all disturbing influences. In the species of animals studied, Magnus did not note any marked change in the motor behaviour if transection was performed at a higher level. For instance, no appreciable difference was apparent whether the basal ganglia were present or absent, though the influence of the optical righting reflexes on posture was noted when the fore-brain was left intact. Some species showed exaggerated righting reflexes after removal of the cerebellum.

Magnus called the righting reflexes: 'General stato-kinetic reactions of the mid-brain or thalamic animal'.

There are five groups of righting reflexes:

1 The labyrinthine righting reflexes on the head.
2 The body righting reflexes acting on the head.
3 The neck righting reflexes.
4 The body righting reflexes acting on the body.
5 The optical righting reflexes.

The labyrinthine righting reflexes on the head

They serve to keep the head in the normal position in space. They were tested in the following manner:

> An animal with intact labyrinths, but blindfolded to exclude righting by vision, was held freely in the air in the normal position. The head then also assumed the normal position. If the pelvis was not turned to the lateral position the head still remained in the normal position. Magnus could turn the pelvis from side to side without affecting the position of the head. Thus the labyrinthine righting reflexes orientate the head in relation to space, the controlling influence being gravity.

The body righting reflexes acting on the head

These reflexes are evoked by the contact of the body surface with the ground. They occur as a result of the asymmetrical stimulation of the tactile sense organs of the body surface.

They were tested in the following manner:

> A thalamic or intact animal without labyrinths (to exclude the effect of the labyrinths righting reflexes on the head) was held freely in the lateral position in the air. It then held its head in the lateral position, owing to the lack of the labyrinthine righting reflex on the head. If the animal was now placed in the lateral position on the table, the head at once assumed the normal position.

The neck righting reflexes

The neck righting reflexes act on the body and serve to keep it in line with the head. On any movement of the head, whether rotation, dorsi- or ventroflexion, while the body remains in the original position, the neck is twisted and this evokes a reflex by which the thorax follows the direction of the head movement. This reflex is the result of stimulation of the proprioceptors of the neck muscles.

Magnus tested this reflex in animals sitting up from the lateral position. He found that after the normal position of the head was restored from the lateral position (as a result of the combined action of the labyrinthine righting reflex and the body righting reflex on the head) the trunk remained in the lateral position, the neck being twisted. This evoked a reflex— the neck righting reflex—by which the thorax was brought into symmetry with the head. There was also a rotation of the lumbar region, which in turn caused a similar reflex upon the hind part of the body, so that finally the whole body followed the head into the normal sitting position. Magnus also observed that dorsiflexion of the head gives rise to lordosis of the spine, and that ventroflexion is followed by a curving of the whole body in the ventral direction.

Brock and Wechsler (1927) described this chain of reflexes as follows:

'As soon as the head rights itself the neck musculature transmits stimuli to the body, bringing the latter into the normal position. Thus a chain of reflex activity starts with the labyrinths or body surface reflexes acting on the head, the head activating the neck musculature, and the latter the axial musculature in a caudal direction.'

The body righting reflexes acting upon the body

These reflexes serve to keep the body in the normal position, even if the head itself is not in the normal position. Like the body righting reflexes acting on the head described above, they are the result of the asymmetrical stimulation of the tactile sense organs of the body surface.

They were tested in the following manner:

A normal animal was held in the lateral position in the air and the head kept firmly in a similar position. The neck righting reflexes then kept the body in the lateral position. When the animal was placed upon a table while the head was kept fixed in the lateral position, the body righted itself into the normal position in spite of the tendency of the neck righting reflexes to keep the body on its side.

The optical righting reflexes

These reflexes are not seen in the thalamic animal since they depend on the integrity of the occipital cortex. In higher mammals such as cats, dogs or monkeys with intact cerebrum, the eyes contribute towards the orientation of the head. Brock and Wechsler (1927) studied apes who had lost the ability to right the head after bilateral labyrinthectomy. They found that the animals compensated for this loss within a fortnight by using the eyes for postural orientation.

Optical righting reflexes play an important role in man. The use of the eyes for postural orientation is a dominant factor in our motor reactions. This can be seen when studying a tabetic patient. The patient begins to sway and fall when he is asked to close his eyes while standing with his feet together (Romberg's sign). The disease process, by interrupting the proprioceptive reflex arc, causes a sensory ataxia. The righting reflexes cannot function properly, but the patient learns to compensate for this loss by fixing his gaze on an object, thus using the optical righting reflexes.

RIGHTING REACTIONS AND THEIR INFLUENCE ON THE MOTOR DEVELOPMENT OF INFANTS AND CHILDREN

The movements of the newborn baby are automatic, and remain so during the first few weeks of life, until gradually cortical control appears (McGraw, 1963).

These early primitive movements called by Egan, Illingworth and MacKeith (1969) 'primary responses' in contrast to 'secondary responses' involve large areas of proximal parts of the body in total flexor or extensor synergies, though during the first few weeks of life isolated movements of distal segments of the limbs and of the mouth are already present. With the maturation of the CNS, secondary responses and new activities appear in a chronological sequence at certain stages of the child's development. The older and more primitive motor patterns are modified; they are partly discarded and partly incorporated into the new patterns. Movements become more varied and differentiated, and smaller segments of the body are moved independently due to the development of inhibitory control. The total flexor and extensor synergies are broken up and resynthesized with many variations of parts of the former total patterns. The succession of these changes is gradual and continuous, extending over the first five years of life. Many of the 'most automatic' motor patterns of postural reactions remain active during adult life. The similarity of motor patterns of different children at the same stage of development has been noted by many workers. Gesell and Amatruda (1949) and Illingworth (1960) have evolved a method of assessment of the developmental age of the children based on their observations.

Schaltenbrand (1925, 1927) has shown that the righting reflexes play an important part in the motor development of the growing infant and child. In contrast to the animal, whose righting reflexes are present at birth and enable it to get on its feet at once, righting reflexes in man are incompletely developed at birth. Only the neck and labyrinthine righting reflexes are then active, while the others make their appearance at certain stages in the child's development. Furthermore, righting reflexes in their unmodified form as described by Magnus on animals, do not persist, but become modified and partly discarded.

The righting reflexes, primitive as they are, enable the child to turn on his side, to roll over to prone lying, to lift his head, to get on hands and knees and to sit. Though the child's early motor behaviour is thus governed by a group of reflexes integrated at a subcortical level, the child soon learns to use these basic patterns of coordination for his voluntary activities.

For an understanding of the movement disorders of patients

with lesions of the central nervous system, a study of the righting reflexes and their development in normal children is essential. As will be discussed later, these patients show either a complete absence of the righting reflexes, or these reflexes are found to be insufficiently developed. In some cases they may be exaggerated and their execution badly coordinated.

Schaltenbrand (1925) describes the results of his investigations of 120 normal children of various ages. The children were examined for postural and movement reactions, and a short survey of his findings follows:

The labyrinth righting reflex on the head

The children were blindfolded (to exclude the optical righting reflexes) and held free in the air (to exclude the body righting reflexes acting on the head). The children were held with both hands around the pelvis and were slowly moved through various positions in space: upright, prone, supine, and sideways to left and to right.

In the newborn baby the labyrinth righting reflex was found to be absent or very weak. The head hung downward, owing to the influence of gravity. In prone and side-lying, jerky movements of the head in the direction of the normal position were sometimes observed, but they were badly sustained and of short duration. They tired quickly and the position of the head could be held at most for a few seconds. During the first few weeks of life the attempts at righting the head became more frequent and more vigorous; they were also noted when the child was in the supine position. But distinct labyrinth righting reflexes on the head were observed only from the second month onwards. The children then tried to bring the head into the normal position— face vertical and mouth horizontal—if placed in any of the above described positions. If the child was moved slowly from one position into the other, the impression was gained that the head remained fixed in the normal position. Schaltenbrand observed the labyrinth righting reflexes on the head in older children also. They were inconstant, however, and he had either to wait for a long time for the reflex to appear, or the effect disappeared after a short time. This inconstancy he ascribed to the older child's ability to inhibit the reflex.

The neck righting reflex

This reflex was found to be present at birth. The child was placed into the supine position and his head was turned to either right or left. This was followed by a reflex rotation of the spine in the direction of the head rotation. If the pelvis was held fixed, the shoulder girdle and trunk followed the head; if the thorax was fixed, the pelvis turned in the opposite direction of the head rotation. This was the form in which Schaltenbrand noted the reflex in the newborn baby. It could, however, be fairly easily elicited in children of three to four years of age. At about fives years of age it become inconstant, and frequently could only be noticed at first examination. At this age the child acquires the ability to inhibit the reflex voluntarily. Paine and Oppé (1966) state:

> 'A phenomenon closely resembling a true neck righting reflex may be demonstrated in the normal newborn infant, in that the examiner can turn the body towards one side by turning the head. However, in the newborn this is a smooth, immediate and almost simultaneous turning based merely on general hypertonus and on close observation is clearly different from the two-phase neck righting reflex seen later in the first year.'

The body righting reflex acting on the head

This reflex could not be studied in children in isolation, as the labyrinth righting reflex on the head acts in close harmony with it. As in animals, the reflex is stimulated by the asymmetrical touch of the body surface with the ground.

The body righting reflex acting on the body

Like the body righting reflex acting on the head, this reflex is evoked by the asymmetrical stimulation of the sensory receptors of the surface of the body. The examination of this reflex is very difficult as it requires the exclusion of vision and of the labyrinths. Though he was unable to study this reflex in isolation, Schaltenbrand observed its activity in the changing sequence of movements of children in getting up from the supine position. The development of the human way of getting up from supine is as follows:

> If an infant is placed flat on his back on a table, the head after a short while turns to the side, and soon afterwards the whole body follows the head (owing to the action of the neck righting reflex). Schaltenbrand remarks that the movement often gave the impression of an active effort of the infant to get on to his side. This is probably due to the increasing element of volition which comes into play after some time of purely reflex turning to the side. The child then uses the pattern of the neck righting reflex voluntarily.

In the second half of the first year children turn more and more often over to prone lying. They mostly turn the head first, then the shoulder girdle and finally the pelvis around the body axis. This already shows a modification of the neck righting reflex by the body righting reflex on the body. The body no longer follows the head movement as a whole, but there is a rotation between shoulder girdle and pelvis on turning to the side, and a further rotation around the body axis, which makes the turning over to the prone position possible. When lying face down, the children lift the head to the normal position, owing to a combination of the labyrinth righting and the body righting reflexes on the head, and they crouch on all fours, a very characteristic position at this age. (In the assumption of this position, the neck righting reflex probably plays a part in producing a lordosis of the spine, and the symmetrical tonic neck reflex its own part in extending the arms and flexing the legs.) In time, children learn to get into the sitting position, and from that posture they finally learn to get on to their legs. If the children are assisted so that they can pull themselves up with their hands to the sitting posture, the rotation around the body axis need not occur.

In this way of getting up, rotation around the body axis is a significant feature and largely due to the body righting reflex on the body, though other righting reflexes such as the neck righting reflex and the labyrinth righting reflex on the head play their part in the sequence of the movement. One can say that a chain of righting reflexes affects the movement. Egan, Illingworth and MacKeith (1969) call this reaction 'rolling response' and say:

> 'If the child is supine and the head is turned, first the hips and lower limbs turn into alignment and then the shoulders and thorax. These trunk-on-head and head-on-trunk righting responses are the basis for rolling.'

About the second and third years a change becomes apparent. The children simplify the transition from supine to sitting by using only partial rotation around the body axis, leaving the pelvis on one side in contact with the support, while pushing themselves up with the arms, mainly on that side of the body. (This means a weakening of the body righting reflexes on the body.) The shoulder girdle, during this phase, is still turned strongly around the body axis. Soon afterwards, the children omit the rotation and develop the adult way of getting up, i.e. the body is symmetrically raised until the sitting position is arrived at, with the help of the arms pushing against the support. (The body righting reflex acting on the body has become inhibited at this stage.) From sitting they get on their feet with a forward movement. This process of development ends at the age of about the fourth to fifth year. Every human being, therefore, goes through a quadrupedal stage, in which the body righting reflexes on the body play an important role, and only slowly is the specific symmetrical human way of getting up developed from the primitive manner.

Schaltenbrand (1925) described a group of reflexes observed in infants and young children which do not belong strictly to the righting reflexes, but which are movement reactions obtained by stimulation of the semicircular canals. Like the righting reflexes, they make their appearance at certain stages of the child's development.

1 The protective extension of the arms (called 'parachute reaction' by Paine and Oppé, 1966).
2 The lift reaction.
3 The Landau reflex.

The 'protective reaction of the arms' (Parachute reaction)

This is a special type of reflex, which is the posture assumed by an animal as it lands at the end of a jump (Brock and Wechsler, 1927). The reaction was observed by Schaltenbrand in older children. The child was held by the trunk freely in the air, and then moved quickly downwards, whereupon the arms extended immediately with abducted and extended fingers. It was suggested by Schaltenbrand that this reaction is the only remnant of the Moro reflex to remain active in adult life. It is the cause of a number of typical injuries, such as abrasions of the palm of the hand. Colles fractures, subluxation of the elbow joint, and fractures of the clavicle. This reaction occurs not only forwards and downwards, but also sideways and backwards. It is a protective reaction against falling and also helps the child to get his trunk balance in sitting. It consists of two phases, (1) the extension of the arm, wrist and fingers for reaching towards the ground or other support, (2) taking weight on the supporting arm and hand. It develops in a forward direction around 6 to 7 months of age, sideways around 8 months and backwards between 10 and 12 months. These protective reactions remain through adult life.

The lift reaction

The lift reaction of the head and of the extremities were first described by Magnus. For examination, the person was placed on hands and knees on a table and the table was then moved upwards and downwards. At the beginning of the movement upwards, the arms bent and the head was lowered; at the end of the movement the arms were straightened and the head lifted. On moving the table downwards the same reaction took place in inverted sequence. Schaltenbrand observed the lift reaction in 50% of all newborn babies. It occurred with regularity only after about 6 months of age.

The 'Landau' reflex

This reflex is a combination of tonic and righting reflexes. It appears about the age of 5 months. Scherzer and Tscharnuter (1982) describe it as follows:

'Head lifting in prone starts a "chain reaction" of extension against gravity. Complete antigravity extension is expressed in the Landau reaction which is obtained between 5 and 8 months and can be observed first in prone and subsequently in ventral suspension. . . . In the Landau reaction, neck and trunk extend and the legs assume a pattern of extension, slight abduction and external rotation of the hips, extension of the knees and, mostly, dorsiflexion of the ankles . . .'

If one lifts a child in prone off the table, supported only by one hand under the thorax, the child will first lift the head so that the face is in the vertical position. This is due to the labyrinth righting reflex on the head. After lifting the head, there occurs a tonic extension of the spine and legs, which can be so strong that the whole body of the child arches backwards. (The extension of the spine on dorsiflexion of the head was ascribed by Schaltenbrand to the influence of symmetrical tonic neck reflexes, while Byers, 1938, interpreted it as a special form of a neck righting reflex.) If, with the child in the extended position, the head is pressed downwards, the extensor tone disappears instantly, and the child folds up like a clasp-knife. Schaltenbrand observed this reflex in its pure form in about 10% of children. He found traces of it in all children between 1 and 2 years of age.

PRIMARY AND SECONDARY REACTIONS

Strictly speaking primary reactions do not belong to the righting and equilibrium reactions, but they are important for assessment of babies and early diagnosis.

In fact, they are a group of innate primary responses that can be elicited in normal babies during the first two months of life which gradually disappear or become part of the so-called secondary responses. Secondary responses appear at the age of 4 to 7 months and in some degree persist. That the primary reactions are not learned but innate can be demonstrated by evoking them before the baby has used them in voluntary activity. All of them have been described by André-Thomas, Dargassies and Chesni (1960) and by Egan, Illingworth and MacKeith (1969). Only those that have some relation to the righting reactions are listed below:

1. Head righting response
2. Primary standing (supporting response)
3. Automatic walking (primary stepping)
4. The Moro reflex (Moro response)
5. Placing reactions (placing response)
6. Incurvation reflex (Galant's reflex)
7. Crossed extension
8. Withdrawal reflex
9. Landau reflex
10. Parachute reaction (precipitation reflex) also called protective reactions
11. Tonic reaction of the finger flexors (finger grasp)
12. Tonic reaction of the toe flexors (toe grasp)
13. Rolling response
14. Balancing reactions

1   Head righting response

'The newborn infant, held vertical, can momentarily keep his head balanced erect. At 10 weeks, in ventral suspension he lifts

his head so that the face is vertical and the mouth horizontal'
(Egan *et al.*, 1969).

2 Primary standing (supporting response)

'The newborn infant is held vertically with the soles of the feet
on the ground; progressive righting of the individual segments
of the lower limbs occurs. The effect can be obtained by standing
the infant on one leg. The stance is firm and should be elicited
on each leg separately. The righting is often inconstant on first
testing for it, and can sometimes be started by passive extension
of the head. In the first 3 to 4 months most infants extend the
lower limbs and will support their weight. In the 4th, 5th and
6th month the response is less vigorous, but from 6 months, it is
normally present again and persists' (Egan *et al.*, 1969).

3 Automatic walking (primary stepping)

'When the newborn infant is held upright with his feet on the
ground and gently moved forward, walking starts and he needs
no more propulsion. Coordination of the walking is good, its
rhythm is regular; the heel is put down first with strong
dorsiflexion of the foot' (André-Thomas *et al.*, 1960). MacKeith
(1964) has found that automatic walking can be evoked by
passive extension of the head after the reaction has disappeared.

4 The Moro reflex (Moro response)

In the first 3 or 4 months, if the supine infant's head is allowed
to drop, there is sudden extension and abduction of the upper
limbs, with opening of the hands, followed by flexion to the
midline. This reflex is a characteristic reaction of infants to a
number of stimuli, such as movement of the supporting surface,
tapping of the abdomen, sudden passive extension of the legs or
blowing of the face. The reaction consists of a movement of
abduction and extension of the arms from their usual flexed
posture. Following this, the arms are frequently adducted at the

shoulders and placed in flexion on the body. At the same time the legs perform a similar movement. (Embracing or 'Umklammerungs' reflex.) Frequently, the extension-abduction phase ends with the assumption of a tonic neck reflex attitude. As early as 1912 Magnus described the strong reaction of the arms when tipping a normal infant backwards. He called this reaction a 'labyrinth reaction' (Bogengang reflex) and showed that it occurs also when the neck is fixed.

The Moro reflex is present during the first 3 months of life, then it becomes weaker, and finally disappears at 6 months of age. Schaltenbrand could elicit the Moro reflex by moving the infant passively, especially by movement of the head. He proved that on holding an infant around the trunk and moving him in a straight line in any one direction in space, extension and abduction of the limbs occurred. He called these responses 'reactions on progressive movements'. The same reaction occurred on rotation and on tipping the child forward, sideways and backwards. The reaction was found to be strongest on tipping backwards. Schaltenbrand suggests that these characteristic movement reactions of the infant should be separated from the collective term 'Moro reflex' and called 'reactions on rotation, tipping and progressive movements'.

André-Thomas, Dargassies and Chesni (1960) state that the Moro reflex becomes weaker, till, at 2 months, it produces only abduction and raising of the arms; the forearms and fingers however, do not extend completely. It appears that the child's ability to right his head against falling backwards, i.e. his flexor activity against gravity, weakens the Moro reflex and inhibits excessive extension of the arms and hands. The Moro reflex is finally inhibited around 6 months of age when the child can support himself forwards on his extended arms, i.e. when he has protective extension of his arms forwards. The 'last remnant of the Moro reflex' may then be seen in the extension and abduction of the child's fingers when reaching out for the ground. The arms no longer fly upwards and backwards, but serve a functional protective purpose.

5 Placing reactions (placing response)

a Placing reaction of the lower limb

'The infant is lifted and the dorsum of one foot is pressed against the edge of the table. The response consists of flexion of different segments of the leg, bringing the foot above the table (first stage) and extension of the limb on active or passive contact of the sole with the table (second stage). This reaction is obtainable after the first 10 days. The second stage develops in the same way as the righting with the feet on the ground' (André-Thomas *et al.*, 1960).

b Placing reaction of the upper limb

'The infant is held up and the back of one of his hands is applied to the under edge of the table. The different segments of the upper limb flex, thus bringing the hand above the table. Complete extension of the limb does not occur until the 3rd or 4th month' (André-Thomas *et al.*, 1960).

It seems that this reaction is superseded by the parachute reaction when the child is about 6 months of age and can see the table in front of him.

6 Incurvation of the trunk (Galant's reflex)

In the suspended position, stimulation of the skin between the twelfth rib and the iliac crest results in lateral flexion of the trunk towards the stimulated side—Galant's reflex—a most constant reflex. According to Galant, this reaction is strongest in the first 2 months and gradually becomes weaker. It is thought to be the remnant of an old, phylogenetic behaviour of the level of amphybians and reptiles (Peiper, 1961, 1963).

7 Crossed extension

Rubbing the sole of the left foot while the left leg is held in extension causes flexion and then extension and adduction of the right leg with extension and fanning of the toes. Crossed extension usually disappears before the end of the first month; at this stage, the leg on the opposite side to the stimulus flexes and remains in this position.

8   Withdrawal reflex

Pricking the sole of the foot causes extension of the toes, dorsiflexion of the foot and flexion of the leg and thigh. There is no need to repeat the stimulus; the reaction is brisk and the latent period short.

9   The Landau reflex

See pages 83–85.

10   Parachute reaction (precipitation reflex)

This is a 'secondary response'. At 6 to 8 months, if held by his trunk and pushed downwards and sideways, the infant moves his upper limbs towards the table, seeking support. The extension of the different segments, fingers included, occurs before contact is made with the table. Contact is made on the palmar surface of the hand; it is strong enough to support the weight of the body and must be evaluated separately with each upper limb. At first the contact is taken on a fisted hand. The forward parachute reaction is present at 6 months, the sideways protective reaction in the sitting position from 6 to 8 months and the backward protective reaction from 10 to 12 months of age.

11   Tonic reaction of the finger flexors (also called finger grasp or grasp reflex)

'Light pressure on the metacarpo-phalangeal groove produces flexion of the fingers; the thumb does not oppose the fingers, but it flexes with them. The reaction is inhibited by repeatedly pricking the palm. It varies from one moment to the next and should not be considered a reflex. If one pulls on an object that the infant is grasping, his grip is strong enough to retain the object, even if the pulling is sufficient to extend the forearm and

arm and partly raise his trunk from the table. If one puts a stick
into the hand of the newborn he grasps it. In this way, he can
hold on to it and the hands can carry the weight of the baby in
the air for a little while. Its duration is sometimes a minute and
longer until he lets go (Peiper, 1961).'

The reflex represents a phylogenetic remnant of the time
when the young held on to the fur of the mother on the
underside of her abdomen, as we can still see in young monkeys.
It is less easy to elicit after 4 to 5 months when voluntary
grasping begins.

12   Tonic reaction of the toe flexors (toe grasp)

The grasp reflex of the toes is elicited by strong pressure on the
ball of the foot. It is followed by tonic flexion of all five toes
which grasp the object. The reflex is weaker than that of the
hand, but always elicitable. It normally persists until 9 to 12
months.

13   Rolling response

This is a secondary response. 'In the newborn period if the
baby's head is rotated, the body tends to follow it around,
rather like a log. As the child grows older, a complicated set of
reactions can be observed as the child is rolled. Derotative
righting, well described by Milani-Comparetti and Gidoni
(1967), begins to develop around the 4th month. If the child is
supine and the head turned, first the hips and lower limbs turn
into alignment and then the shoulders and thorax. These trunk-
on-head righting responses are the basis for rolling' (Egan *et al.*,
1969).

14   Balancing reactions

These are also secondary responses. They keep the head and
body properly orientated in space; causing the head to 'right'
itself and the body to come into line with it. Sideways balance is
tested by holding the child erect and tilting him to one side. At 4

months old, he will tilt his head to 30° to keep his eyes level. At 5 months, the spine curves to aid in the compensatory adjustment, but the baby who shows these reactions when held up and tilted does not use them when he is first placed in a sitting position.

The presence of righting reflexes in patients depends largely on the state of postural tone. The release of tonic reflexes in conjunction with a state of abnormally increased muscle tone will have a severe inhibitory effect on the stato-kinetic reactions.

This view is supported by Schaltenbrand (1927) who has studied the effect of the release of the abnormal postural reflexes on the motor behaviour of patients with cerebral damage. He classified the patients into two groups according to the severity of the damage.

The first syndrome, the more severe one, he called 'complete decerebrate rigidity, characterized by extremely primitive postural reflexes'. It consists of:

1 Increase of muscle tone
2 Unequal distribution of tone with predilection for the anti-gravity muscles
3 Tonic neck and tonic labyrinthine reflexes acting on the extremities
4 The Moro reflex (normally present in babies under 3 months of age)
5 Loss of righting reflexes
6 Increased tendon reflexes.

The second syndrome he regarded as evidence of a somewhat less devastating injury to the motor system, and he called it 'the quadrupedal syndrome'. It consists of:

1 Positive neck righting reflexes (normally present in infants)
2 The primitive form of getting up and inability to sit up symmetrically

3 Difficulty in standing upright (not because of local muscular weakness)

4 Impairment of finer voluntary movements.

In comparing these two syndromes we can see that the essential difference lies in the presence of tonic reflexes with loss of righting reflexes in patients of the first group, while righting reflexes are present in those of the second group. The opinion that the released tonic reflexes inhibit stato-kinetic reflexes is borne out by our observations on patients under treatment. If one succeeds in inhibiting the abnormal tonic reflex activity and with it in reducing hypertonus in patients who show the first syndrome, righting reactions either occur spontaneously or can be facilitated by special techniques of treatment. This proves the interesting fact that even in very severe cases, higher reactions are often potentially present. They can be freed from the inhibition imposed upon them by the action of abnormally strong tonic reflexes. Treatment often succeeds in freeing righting reactions in patients of the first group, thus bringing them into the second group. Severe cases of the first group, could be advanced to the quadrupedal stage. They learnt to kneel, to crawl normally, and to sit and use their hands. Normal standing and walking, however, could usually not be obtained in these cases, probably because the equilibrium reactions were totally absent. In those patients who showed the second, less severe syndrome, equilibrium reactions could usually be facilitated, and the patients could learn to stand and walk in a normal or fairly normal manner.

The examination of individual righting reactions in patients presents great difficulties, as they interact closely with each other. Moreover, as they are only present in the lighter cases who are able to perform voluntary movements, the picture becomes more complex. The division between the light and the severe cases is not as clear-cut as the table by Schaltenbrand suggests. There are cases that fall between these two groups, and show tonic reflex activity of moderate strength or a transient character, and frequently one or other of the righting reactions.

TESTING OF RIGHTING REACTIONS

Some of the individual righting reactions can be tested fairly easily.

The labyrinth righting reaction on the head was tested with the child held free in the air in the manner described by Schaltenbrand. The position of the head was noted while moving the child through various positions in space. (The action of the optical righting reactions was not excluded by blindfolding the child.) Another way of testing was to note the patient's ability to raise the head while lying prone, or supine, or in the young child his ability to control his head when pulled to sitting.

The neck righting reaction was tested in the supine position, the patient's head being turned to the side and his response noted. If the reflex was present, shoulder and pelvis followed the head.

The body righting reaction on the body was tested by asking the patient to turn from supine to prone lying, and to get on hands and knees. Special note was taken as to whether the body as a whole followed the rotation of the head to one side— the usual initiation of the turning movement—or whether there was rotation between shoulder girdle and pelvis, the latter rotation being due to the influence of the body righting reaction on the body. Another way of testing this reaction was to ask the patient to stand up from the supine position. Note was made of the manner in which he accomplished this.

The Landau reflex was tested with the child held free in the air as described by Schaltenbrand. Older children, who because of their weight could not be tested in this way, were held by the pelvis, the examiner standing astride, with the patient's legs between his own and his body hanging free in the air. If the Landau reflex was present, the patient raised his head and trunk, and extended the hips in the manner described.

The **'protective extension of the arms'** was tested in the same positions as the Landau reflex, tilting of the head towards the ground. If the reaction was present the patient extended his arms and hands towards the support (Figs 8.1; 8.2). This reaction was also tested in the sitting posture by pushing the patient to one side and observing whether he extended the arm and hand on that side to prevent himself from falling over (Figs 8.3; 8.4). In children who could sit on their heels the reaction could be tested by pushing their trunk forward. If the reaction was present, the patient spontaneously stretched out his arms and hands in order to protect himself from falling on his face.

The testing of patients for the presence or absence of postural reflexes, both static and stato-kinetic, gives a fairly reliable picture of the severity of the individual case and of the residual motor activity of the patient. Furthermore, it will indicate his

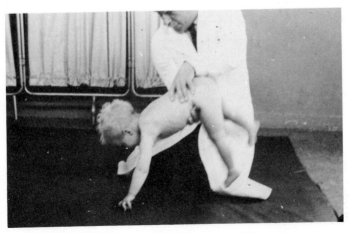

Fig 8.1 Normal protective extension of the arms.

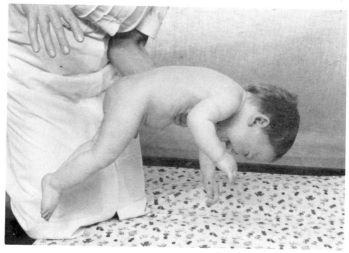

Fig 8.2   Absence of protective extension of the arms.

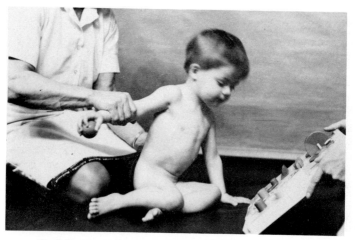

Fig 8.3   Normal protective extension of the arm sideways.

needs as regards to treatment and be of great value in assessing his progress.

As already mentioned, there is a close relationship between the state of postural tone and the presence of righting reflexes. In most patients with severe degrees of spasticity, righting reactions and equilibrium reactions are absent. In some of these patients we found one or other of the righting reflexes active, but all the rest inhibited by the abnormal strength of tonic reflexes. Thus, the labyrinthine righting reflex on the head could be observed in a few cases with severe extensor spasticity of trunk, neck and legs. In these patients extensor activity was pronounced even in the prone position, in which tonic labyrinthine reflexes usually produce flexor spasticity. It appeared as if this extensor activity in prone lying facilitated the labyrinth righting reaction on the head. The child not only raised his head spontaneously when placed in the prone position, but held it up for a long time, the extensors of the neck offering considerable resistance to passive flexion and the head being

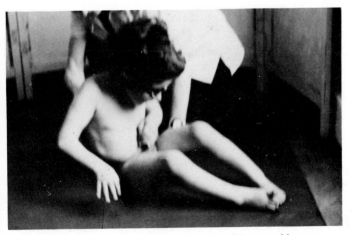

Fig 8.4 Absence of protective extension of the arm sideways.

slowly raised again when released. These patients, however, were unable—except possibly for a second—to lift their heads when in the supine position, since the labyrinth righting reaction on the head was inhibited by the severe extensor spasticity of neck and trunk in this position (tonic labyrinthine influence).

Some children with severe degrees of flexor spasticity persisting even in the supine position (in which extensor spasticity is usually dominant) showed positive neck righting reactions while all other righting reactions were absent. In these cases, flexor spasticity seemed to facilitate the neck righting reaction, i.e. the automatic turning of the body to the side from the supine position after turning the face to that side.

Righting reactions are usually present in cases with moderate degrees of spasticity, but they are weak and often delayed, probably owing to the inhibiting influence of the increased muscle tone. Such patients move very slowly and frequently remain for long periods in the uncomfortable and abnormal position into which they may have been placed for testing. They usually have some capacity for willed movements which they can use to compensate for the inadequate automatic righting mechanism. The attempts at maintaining balance by voluntary activity are, however, insufficient when changes in the patient's equilibrium are quick, sudden and unexpected. These patients seem to have to 'think' of every movement; they move cautiously and they restrict themselves to the few movements which they know to be safe. They are afraid, for instance, to use their arms and hands freely in sitting, or to look around in standing and walking.

Righting reactions are usually present in patients with spasticity and involuntary movements, or spasticity with ataxia. In these cases, tonic reflexes are pronounced in certain positions that favour their occurrence, but less strong in other positions or under conditions of reduced stimulation. Righting reactions may then be active but are interfered with and arrested by the sudden action of the tonic reflexes. Movements initiated by the righting reactions are suddenly stopped and the patient becomes fixed in a tonic spasm.

In the cases of pure athetosis and ataxia, which show hypotonicity, righting reactions are active and may be exaggerated, but their initiation is usually delayed, probably owing to the reduced responsiveness of hypotonic muscles. The course of their execution is lacking in precision of range, timing and direction. Because of the postural instability, resulting from too low a muscle tone, and the insufficient grading of contraction and relaxation of antagonists, the movements are jerky and uncontrolled. Thus righting and equilibrium reactions become the cause of loss of balance instead of serving their purpose of maintaining it.

The labyrinth righting reaction on the head

This reaction was tested in the prone position and was observed in most patients with moderate or slight degrees of spasticity. In athetoid patients the righting movements often led to rigid hyperextension of the neck alternating with complete collapse into flexion. In ataxic patients the movements were usually weak and often incomplete in range, and the erect position could not be maintained. In the supine position the labyrinth righting reaction on the head was absent in most patients, even in a large number of those with active reactions in the prone position. We tested the reaction by lowering the trunk of the patient from the sitting posture to supine. Few patients, spastic, athetoid or ataxic, kept their faces in the vertical position before their shoulders touched the ground. The head usually dropped back at some stage during the backward movement of the body. The normal reaction, of holding up the head until the shoulder girdle touches the support, was only present in patients whose upper extremities were little or not at all affected, exceptions being a few severely spastic patients whose spasticity was predominantly in the flexor muscles of the trunk, neck and arms. In these patients, the excess of flexor tone could still be noticed in the supine position where usually extensor tone predominated. Though they usually did not show active labyrinth righting reactions in the prone position, they seemed unable to keep their head down on the support when lying on their back. The head kept 'bobbing up' constantly as if the child wanted to look for something. In these cases abnormally increased flexor tone seemed to facilitate the righting movement of the head in supine.

The neck righting reaction

This reaction was tested in supine and was always absent in patients with severe extensor spasticity of neck and trunk. It was inhibited by the combined influence of tonic neck and tonic labyrinthine reflexes which in these patients were usually very active. Pronounced asymmetrical tonic neck reflexes occurred on turning the head to the side, a movement which should initiate a neck righting reaction. In most cases the tonic neck reflex was more active on turning the head to one side, usually to the right. These patients often showed a positive neck righting reaction on turning the face to the left side. Turning the head to the right side, however, led to an extension of the jaw arm with protraction of that shoulder, and flexion of the skull arm with abduction and strong retraction of the shoulder. This latter, combined with the extensor spasticity in the supine position (due to the tonic labyrinthine reflex) prevented the left shoulder and thorax from following the movement of the head (inhibition of the neck righting reaction). Thus the patient was unable to turn from supine to the right side.

We found neck righting reactions active in a great number of young children who showed little extensor spasticity. They usually failed to show asymmetrical tonic neck reflexes, or if these were present, they were transient and weak. These children appeared to be 'flaccid' rather than spastic, until their reactions to passive extension were examined when they showed abnormally increased flexor tone (Fig. 8.5).

A few children, mostly of the athetoid type whose legs were less affected than their arms, managed to turn from the supine

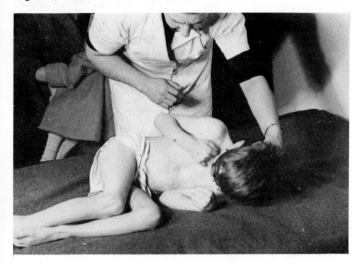

Fig 8.5

position to the side by flexing the legs and rotating the pelvis to the side to which they wanted to turn. Though rigid extension of neck and spine, with a tonic neck reflex acting on the arms (as described above) prevented the normal sequence of the movement of the thorax in following the head to the side, this movement could occur after the necessary flexion and rotation had been obtained by the movement of the legs.

It is interesting to note that the neck righting reaction was still strongly active in a few children above the age of 6 years in whom it should normally have disappeared. They showed slight spasticity and were of the hyperkinetic type and often mentally retarded. They could walk and run and use their hands, but their actions were clumsy and they were unable to perform fine movements. Their motor patterns were those of children of 3 to 4 years of age.

The body righting reaction on the body

This reaction was present in all patients with moderate

spasticity and in athetoid and ataxic patients: Rotation between
pelvis and thorax being essential for this reaction, the patient
with moderate spasticity could usually rotate his thorax against
his pelvis, while athetoid and ataxic patients could rotate the
pelvis against the thorax. Though all these patients could roll
over from supine to prone lying, only a few of them could get on
hands and knees and crawl. Children with severe extensor
spasticity and with active labyrinth righting reflexes on the
head experienced great difficulty in turning over from supine to
the side, owing to the inhibition of the neck righting reflex (by
extensor spasticity in supine and tonic neck reflex activity).
After they were helped to turn on to their side, however, they
could complete the movement of turning over to prone, since
the labyrinth righting reflex on the head enabled them to raise
it, and extensor tone in the trunk and hips was, even in the
prone position, sufficiently strong to allow them to lie extended
on their stomachs. By contrast, children with marked flexor
spasticity, even in the supine position, could turn to the side,
since the neck righting reflex was active, but the increase of
flexor spasticity in prone lying (due to the tonic labyrinthine
reflexes) produced such a degree of flexion of the arms, trunk
and hips that turning over to prone was quite impossible. They
could neither lift the head into the normal position nor extend
the spine and hips sufficiently to lie flat on the support.

The Landau reflex

This reflex was only observed by us in children with strong
labyrinth righting reflex on the head, i.e. in those children who
could lift the head well in prone and maintain it in that position
with ease (Figs 8.6; 8.7). All these children could sit with an
erect spine and support their body-weight in standing. However, they were usually unable to keep their balance in standing
or walking unaided, but their arms were much less affected
than their legs. In most of these patients the sitting posture
was too stiff and the sitting balance therefore insecure. Passive
flexion of the neck was often strongly resisted, and if this was

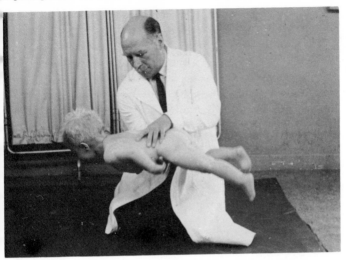

Fig 8.6 Normal Landau reaction.

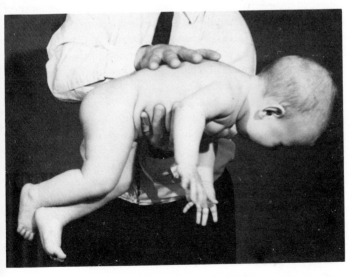

Fig 8.7 Absence of Landau reaction.

attempted in standing, the legs flexed and the children collapsed.

The Landau reaction was absent in all those children who showed tonic reflexes to a marked degree. In these cases extensor spasticity was pronounced in supine, but increase of tone in the flexor muscles was equally strong when the children were in the prone position or held freely in the air, face downwards. They were unable to lift the head or could do so only for a few seconds; the spine did not extend and the legs remained flexed at the hips.

The Landau reaction was absent in all those children who showed pronounced flexor spasticity in all positions. They lacked the extensor tone necessary for this reaction.

The 'protective reaction of the arms' (Parachute reaction)

This reaction was found to be negative in all children with severe degrees of spasticity and hyperactive tonic neck reflexes. Some of these patients showed extension of the arms when their head was raised either in the prone or kneeling position. This extension of the arms, however, was not a true 'protective extension of the arms' but a tonic extension of the elbows with closing of the hand and fingers due to the action of the symmetrical tonic neck reflex.

The 'protective reaction of the arms' was also absent in all patients with marked flexor spasticity of the upper extremities and trunk, and also in the affected arm of the hemiplegic patient.

The reaction was present in all children with moderate spasticity, especially in those whose upper extremities were little or not affected, and in some athetoid and ataxic patients. However, in spastic children the parachute reaction was better developed forwards than sideways, while athetoid and ataxic children showed better reactions sideways than forwards. Very few children had developed them backwards. The ability to support the body-weight on the extended arms was absent or poor in all children even if they were able to reach out for the support. In some of the athetoid patients, if they were held freely in the air face downwards, one could observe a normal reaction with extension of the arms and spreading of fingers, but alternating with flexion.

Most children with a positive 'protective reaction of the arms' could crawl, that is to say that they could support some of their body-weight on their arms and hands.

The Moro reflex (Startle reaction)

This reflex was usually observed in spastic and athetoid quadruplegic patients who had insufficient or absent head control, i.e. the head tended to fall backwards and the patient could not right the head when made to sit up from supine. It also occurred in patients who had some head control when pulled to sitting and who could sit but not balance. They sat with much flexion of the head and spine, but had no protective

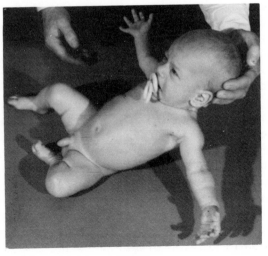

Fig 8.8

extension of the arms and hands. In these cases, as well as in the older and more severely affected quadruplegic children who could sit unsupported, one could observe the second stage of the Moro reflex without full extension of arms and hands. Positions favouring extensor spasticity also seemed to favour the occurrence of the Moro reflex (Fig 8.8).

The reflex was strong in those children who were hypersensitive to noise and touch. They showed marked extensor spasms combined with a Moro reflex, often followed by an asymmetrical tonic neck reflex attitude, on sudden stimulation. The Moro reflex was also active in some milder cases of the hypersensitive type, even in a few patients who could stand and walk a few steps with help, but had insufficient standing and walking balance. They would suddenly extend their legs rigidly, stand on their toes, throw the head backwards, and abduct and lift the arms. They were, however, quite safe from this reaction in kneeling, crawling and sitting.

The trunk incurvation reflex (Galant's reflex)

This reflex normally disappears during the 2nd month, but Ingram (1962) observed it in 3 month-old babies. We found it present in much older children with cerebral palsy, even in a few teenagers. They all had trunk instability and pronounced postural asymmetries. It occurred mainly in the dystonic types of quadruplegic cerebral palsy.

It prevented the children from gaining a stable erect posture against gravity, head control and the use of both hands in midline. In some cases, the incurvation of the trunk was stronger on one side than the other and in a few cases was only present on one side. In these latter cases, it contributed to the development of scoliosis. It usually interacts with asymmetrical tonic neck reflexes.

Interaction of Tonic Reflexes and Righting Reactions

These observations show clearly that there is a relationship between the tonic reflexes and righting reactions, these either reinforcing or inhibiting each other. Even in severe cases tonic reflex activity does not always completely inhibit all the righting reflexes but, in fact, serves to enhance the activity of one or the other. For instance, there is a close relationship between the labyrinth righting reflex on the head and extensor spasticity, and between the neck righting reflex and flexor spasticity; they seem to reinforce each other. But the persistence of tonic reflex activity on abnormal strength interferes with the full development and harmonious interaction of the righting reflexes, and inhibits most, if not all, of these, and all equilibrium reactions.

Similar observations have been made by Pollock and Davies (1927) in decerebrate animals. They produced decerebration by a technique which led to a physiological transection of the neuraxis at a higher level than that of Sherrington's experiments. They thus produced a decerebrate animal with flexor rigidity of the fore-limbs (Kangaroo posture) in contrast to Sherrington's animals which showed extensor rigidity of all limbs. In these animals Pollock and Davies observed an interaction of partially intact righting reflexes with tonic reflexes. They state:

'It is obvious that the labyrinthine-, neck- and body-righting reflexes were not totally intact. Parts of each, however, must have functioned. Although the animals were unable while lying on the abdomen to hold the head in a normal position, they attempted to assume a ventral position when placed on their backs. . . . When righting and tonic or standing reflexes are destroyed in otherwise

normal animals, flexor patterns predominate. When righting reflexes are only partially destroyed in a decerebrate animal both
flexor and extensor rigidity may be produced by suitable stimulation. When the righting reflexes are absent in a decerebrate animal
labyrinthine tonic reflexes predominate and extensor rigidity
occurs.'

A study of the case histories of children with cerebral palsy
reveals the interesting fact that even in severe cases some
righting reflexes must have been present in early infancy, and
that these early righting reflexes must have been lost at some
stage of the child's development. This can be explained by the
well-known fact that most children with cerebral palsy do not
show appreciable degrees of spasticity during the first months of
life, making an early diagnosis very difficult. They may even
seem 'flaccid' at first, with spasticity developing only gradually
later on. Occasionally, it may appear only when the child is put
on his feet, whereas up to this point he may have seemed quite
normal. In a few lighter cases cerebral palsy may be diagnosed
only after a child has started to walk. This point is borne out by
the following summary of a case history:

> A child suffering from a spastic paraplegia, with very slight
> involvement of the hands, had a normal twin, and the mother could
> therefore easily compare the motor behaviour of the two children.
> Up to the quadrupedal stage, there was, according to the mother, no
> difference in the development of the two. The spastic child even
> started to walk of her own accord, but with abnormal coordination.
> Then the legs became stiff, and the child walked on her toes and
> could not keep her balance. It was at this point that the mother
> consulted a doctor for the first time.

Righting and equilibrium reactions were sufficiently and
normally active up to the walking stage and tonic reflex activity
was under control. Her CNS could not, however, cope with the
difficult task of balancing on her feet and at this stage tonic
reflexes became exaggerated. The positive supporting reaction
stiffened her legs and prevented her heels from coming down,

and adductor spasticity increased with inward rotation of her legs. This interfered with the development of normal equilibrium reactions.

The strength and distribution of spasticity may change even in older patients. The repeated performance of motor skills, using abnormal patterns of movement, will increase spasticity permanently in certain muscle groups. The same thing may happen if patients remain in certain positions for long periods. For instance, patients who spend their life in the sitting posture may, in time, show flexor deformities in the hips and knees.

A few histories of typical cases may serve to illustrate these points:

1   Patient C.T., aged 2 years when first seen. Congenital spastic quadruplegia of a severe degree.

Unable to turn from supine to the side, roll over to prone, sit without support, stand or walk. Marked asymmetrical tonic neck reflexes to the left, absent on turning the head to the right. Could grasp an object with the right hand, not with the left.

In supine: considerable extensor spasticity, especially of the legs, which frequently showed typical scissor posture. *In prone and when supported in sitting*: marked flexor spasticity of neck, trunk and hips. Unable to raise her head in prone. She hated to be placed into the prone position, and could not hold her head up for a moment after it was passively lifted and released.

Photographs of the same child at the age of 6 months showed her lying prone with the head well raised. This ability disappeared when the child was made to sit with support, owing to the general increase of flexor spasticity produced in sitting.

2   Patient T.R. first seen at age of 3 years 6 months. Severe congenital spastic quadruplegia.

In supine: strong extensor spasticity of neck, trunk and legs, arms retracted at shoulders, head retracted and resisting passive flexion.

Unable to lift head or turn to side in supine. Marked asymmetrical tonic neck reflexes on turning head to right more than to left.

In prone: extensor spasticity, though weaker, still marked. Head lifted spontaneously, held erect and resisted passive flexion.

Unable to roll over from supine to prone, but could complete the movement if being helped into the side-lying position.

Unable to kneel, stand or walk.

When put on his feet, he showed marked extension of the legs with adduction (scissor posture).

If made to sit with support, he showed extension of spine and neck, resisting passive flexion of the neck. Mother states that the child was 'floppy' until 18 months of age and able to lift his head in supine (no information could be obtained as to the chid's ability to turn on side from supine). The child grew stronger and stiffer and lost the ability to raise the head in supine.

3 Patient P.A., 11 years of age when first seen. Severe congenital spastic quadruplegia.

Almost rigid because of severe spasticity of both flexor and extensor muscles of trunk and legs, flexor tone predominating in the trunk, extensor tone in the legs.

Arms showed marked flexor contractures of elbows and wrists, though he could use his fingers to some extent. He lifted his head well in supine but not in prone. Adductor neurectomy, elongation of hamstrings and tendo-achilles was performed on both legs between the age of 4 to 7 years.

Photographs taken before the age of 3 years showed no adductor spasm or other abnormality of the legs. Mother states that there was nothing abnormal in the arms up to 3 years of age. He crawled well at this age.

Between 3 and 4 years of age a typical scissor posture development in the legs, with adductor spasm, flexion of knees and plantiflexion of the feet.

After the operations the patient learned to walk with the help of two sticks. The legs were then in abduction and rigidly extended at the knees, the left more than the right. The right leg was placed forward in a step, the left one drawn forward to the level of the right. The trunk was flexed at the hips to a near right-angle. When examined at 11 years of age, the patient was unable to lie prone and lift his head in this position. This was due to the spastic contraction of the flexor muscles of neck, trunk, hips and arms. He could turn to his side. He could not be placed on hands and knees, as he could not flex his legs or support his weight on his hands. He was unable to crawl. The 'protective reaction of the arms' was absent.

In addition to having developed flexor contractures of the arms, this child had lost a number of righting reactions which must have been present at an earlier age, e.g. the labyrinth righting reflex on the head, the protective reaction of the arms and the body righting reflex on the body. This happened at the age when he tried to stand and walk.

The evolution of the upright posture in man has necessitated the development of a reflex mechanism serving the function of maintaining and regaining balance in standing and walking. This mechanism consists of a group of automatic reactions which Weisz (1938) called 'equilibrium reactions'. They are of a more complex nature that the righting reflexes and are specific to man. The level of integration of these reflexes is not known, but they probably need cortical control for their function. Weisz' study of the equilibrium reactions was pursued as an extension of those made by Magnus on postural reflexes. They have not, however, been studied as extensively as have the righting reflexes, and are still imperfectly understood. Weisz himself stresses that there may be many more reactions than those found by his manner of investigation.

The equilibrium reactions are elicited by stimulation of the labyrinths. They are compensatory movements, occurring automatically and rendering equilibrium possible. They provide, according to Weisz, for the adaptation of the whole body to the supporting surface, or in other words to a change of the centre of gravity in the body, and to changes in the position of the extremities in relation to the trunk. The reactions assure the proper posture of the body when a change occurs in the supporting surface (as when tipping the table on which the patient is placed) which leads to a change in the centre of gravity of the body. They belong therefore to the stato-kinetic reflexes as conceived by Magnus. They can only occur when postural tone is normal, i.e. sufficiently low to permit a 'readiness' for compensatory movements, but sufficiently high to give proper support tonus.

Weisz investigated the equilibrium reactions by placing a

child on a table and then tipping the table sideways with the child in the prone, supine, sitting, kneeling and standing positions.

In supine and prone the reactions to tipping were analogous. He noticed a stretching out of the extremities, i.e. an increase of support tonus, to the side of the tipping. In sitting, the arms were extended and abducted, and braced against the support. The trunk and head were rotated towards the upper part of the table, the movement being accompanied by a spreading of the legs. In the standing position the upper leg was bent at hip and knee, the other one stiffly extended. Head and trunk were turned towards the raised part of the table. The reactions in the quadrupedal position were similar to those in standing. Increase of support tonus with extension and slight abduction occurred in the extremities near the lower part of the table, and decrease of support tonus with displacement of the weight to the opposite side in the extremities near the raised part of the table.

As a supplement to the reactions to tipping in the standing position, Weisz described the 'see-saw' reaction. He tested it by passively lifting, for example, the left leg, while pushing the body-weight of the child to the left side, i.e. in the direction of the lifted leg. He noticed then a strong extension and abduction of that leg.

Weisz (1938) investigated the equilibrium reactions of 67 children of varying ages. He found they were not present at birth and could not be observed before the age of 6 months. From then onwards they became active, first in prone, then in supine, and later in sitting, kneeling and standing. If they were absent, the children could not maintain the initial position, but fell over towards the lower side of the table if it was tipped. The appearance of the equilibrium reactions occurred in a chronological order which overlapped with that of the righting reflexes. They probably play an important role in the modification of the righting reflexes during the change from the quadrupedal to the adult symmetrical form of getting up.

It is interesting to follow Weisz' observations on the relationship of equilibrium reactions and the learning to sit, stand and walk in normal children.

The first positive results of tipping the infants in the supine and prone positions were observed at about 6 months of age. No positive results were seen in infants sitting and standing at that age. The children who showed positive reactions could already sit with support. They usually showed positive results in the prone position, but only suggestive reactions in supine. Of two twins of 8 months of age, the stronger child exhibited positive reactions both in prone and supine, the weaker one only in prone and suggestive reactions in supine.

Children of 12 months of age showed all positive reactions in lying. They could sit unsupported and most of them could stand without support. In those who could stand, the results in sitting were also positive, whereas those unable to stand without support showed negative reactions in sitting. The tipping in the standing position produced positive results only in a minority of children who were able to stand without support. The see-saw reaction was already present in all children.

At 15 months of age all reactions in lying and sitting were positive. The reaction to tipping in standing, though positive in all children, was uncertain and inconstant. All children could stand and some could make steps with support.

From 18 months to 2 years of age all reactions were positive, but varied in security. All children were able to walk. From then onwards the reactions became more secure, and in older children were carried out with manifest ease.

Thus we see an interesting relationship between the equilibrium reactions and the development of the child's ability to sit, stand and walk. The equilibrium reactions in supine and prone lying become positive only when the child has learned to sit unsupported. They appear in sitting when the child can already stand, and in standing when he can already walk. It appears from this that the perfecting of an equilibrium reaction does not take place until the child has advanced a stage beyond it. From

NORMAL DEVELOPMENT OF POSTURAL REACTIONS

MONTHS	1	2	3	4	5	6	7	8	9	10	11	12	24
Moro	+	+	+	±	very weak	very weak							
Placing reaction of legs	+	+	+	+	+	+							
Placing reaction of arms			+	+	+	+							
Assym. TNR influence	±	+	+	±									
Primary standing	+	+											
Automatic walking	+	+											
Grasp reflex: (a) hands	+	+	+	±									
(b) feet	+	+	+	+	+	+	+	+					
Suckling	+	+	+	±									
Neck righting	+	+	+	+	±	±	±	±	±	±	±		
Body righting on body (derotative)						+	+	+	+	+	+	±	±
Labyrinth righting *(plus optical righting)*	±	+	+	+	+	+	+	+	+	+	+	+	+
Landau				±	±	+	+	+	+	+	+	+	±
Lift reaction						+	+	+	+	+	+	+	+
'Parachute' (prot. extension) (a) forwards						+	+	+	+	+	+	+	+
(b) sideways						+	+	+	+	+	+	+	+
(c) backwards									+	+	+	+	+
Equilibrium reactions Supine							+	+	+	+	+	+	+
Prone						+	+	+	+	+	+	+	+
Sitting								+	+	+	+	+	+
Quadrupedal									+	+	+	+	+
See-saw reaction												±	+
Standing												±	+

Plus = present
Plus/Minus = weak or occasional

the point of view of treatment it means that one should not insist on perfecting one activity before progressing to the next one.

It has been mentioned before that the development of the equilibrium reactions overlaps with that of the righting reflexes. The former are, among other factors, responsible for the modification and transformation of the latter. From the clinical aspect their importance in learning to sit, stand and walk is noteworthy. It is most probable that the righting reflexes in their simple form will not enable a patient to get beyond the quadrupedal stage of motor activity, and that the equilibrium reactions are essential for any activity beyond this stage. Weisz (1938) says:

'There is no doubt that the body righting reflexes gradually fade away in the course of the child's development. Whether they actually disappear or are only suppressed is difficult to decide. It is a matter of fact, however, that parallel to this progress the equilibrium reactions, which are absent at birth, increase in strength and importance. It would seem that we deal here with two synergic phenomena which alternate in their manifestation.'

The chart on p. 97 shows the inhibition of the primary reactions by the righting reactions. From the 6th month of life onwards these are gradually modified and incorporated into the parachute and equilibrium reactions and remain throughout adult life.

The Equilibrium Reactions as Observed on Patients

Weisz (1938) found equilibrium reactions present in cases of cerebellar ataxia. He found that fundamentally these patients showed the same group of reactions of a compensatory nature as healthy adults, but the movements ensued briskly and hypermetrically, were imperfectly inhibited and sometimes occurred after a delay. The reactions, while primarily present, became secondarily modified in the course of their execution. He saw the disturbance not in the inability to maintain equilibrium, but in the regulation of the required movements.

We have made similar observations in patients suffering from ataxia and athetosis. In both types of cases righting and equilibrium reactions are present, but their action is interfered with, and the movements misdirected and uncoordinated. This seems to us to be largely owing to the instability of muscle tone in ataxic and athetoid patients. Muscle tone fluctuates suddenly between hypo- and hypertonicity, and the contraction of muscles and the relaxation of their antagonists is abrupt and shows a lack of grading. Treatment by stabilizing and normalizing muscle tone results in the disappearance of involuntary movements and ataxia. Righting and equilibrium reactions can then act normally.

We examined the equilibrium reactions by noting the reactions of patients following disturbance of their balance by displacement of the centre of gravity in sitting (Fig 11.1), kneeling, and standing (Figs 11.2; 11.3). We did not test them in supine or prone lying.

The equilibrium reactions were absent in all cases with severe degrees of spasticity. In the sitting and kneeling postures, they were present in patients with slight spasticity in ataxics and in

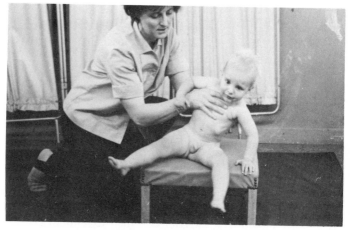

Fig 11.1   Normal equilibrium reaction in sitting.

Fig 11.2   Normal equilibrium reaction in standing.

Fig 11.3 Absence of equilibrium reaction in standing.

athetoids. They were observed only in children who could crawl in a fairly normal manner, and who could sit and use their hands. They were inconstant and frequently interfered with by tonic spasms or involuntary movements. This happened especially if the centre of gravity was displaced too suddenly or too far in any direction.

Equilibrium reactions in standing were present in a few athetoid and ataxic children who could walk fairly normally. They were rarely present in spastic children, even if these could walk, which they did with abnormal coordination. The see-saw reaction was absent in most children. Some children extended the raised leg, but collapsed on the standing leg. Most of the children did not extend the raised leg when the weight was transferred towards that side: they flexed both legs and sat down.

There is no doubt that there are many more reactions opposing displacement of the centre of gravity, similar to the equilibrium reactions, described by Weisz. We observed with regularity the following reaction to displacement of the centre of gravity backwards in standing:

On tipping a normal standing person unexpectedly back-wards (standing behind him with one's arms around his trunk under his armpits), we could observe a spontaneous dorsiflexion of the feet at the ankles so that the front of the foot was lifted off the ground (Fig 11.4). This reaction is positive in every normal person if care is taken to prevent him from taking a step backwards in order to regain his balance. We found this reaction absent in all spastic patients with appreciable degrees of extensor spasticity of the legs. If extensor spasticity is moderate, the toes may lift off the ground but the ankles do not dorsiflex (Fig 11.5).

All these patients were unable to walk placing the heel to the ground first (heel-toe walk). Most of the patients with severe extensor spasticity were unable to put the heel down at all,

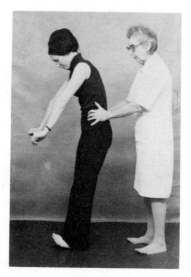

Fig 11.4

Fig 11.5

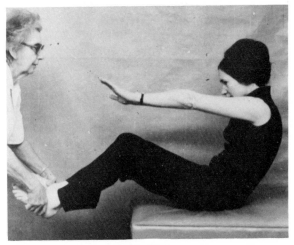

Fig 11.6

while those with moderate extensor spasticity were often able to place the heel down after touching the ground with the toes first. In athetoid and ataxic patients the reaction was often present, but inconstant.

Another reaction of a similar nature could be observed in a flexion forward at the shoulder joint of the extended arms, following displacement of the body-weight backwards in sitting and standing (Fig 11.6). This reaction is always absent in patients with marked extensor spasticity of the trunk and retraction of the arms at the shoulder.

From the point of view of treatment, the facilitation of normal equilibrium reactions in all activities is an essential preparation for standing and walking.

12   Summary and Conclusions

Postural reflexes as well as normal postural reaction have been described in isolation, and the influence of their combined action on the motor behaviour of patients has been analyzed. Their appearance and modification in the maturing infant and child has been followed. It has been stressed that these postural reactions and their harmonious interaction formed the background of normal voluntary movements and skills, and that without their full development and integration normal motor activities could not be expected.

The disorders of posture and movement of patients with lesions of the central nervous system were seen as being largely due to a disorganization or arrest of the development of the postural reflex mechanism. The degree of the release of tonic reflexes, resulting in an inhibition of higher postural reflex activity, appeared to be in direct proportion to the severity of the individual case. Though the abnormal patterns of the released tonic reflexes could only be observed clearly in severely spastic patients, similar abnormal reaction patterns could be seen in cases with moderate or slight spasticity and in ataxic and athetoid patients. In the latter, involuntary movements obscured the typical patterns. In spite of this, the underlying uniformity of postural patterns was found to be striking.

The testing of patients for the presence or absence of normal or abnormal postural reactions was found to be useful in assessing the severity of the individual case and of the patient's residual motor ability. It was also found helpful in the planning of treatment and in assessing improvement (Bobath, K. 1969; 1980).

A treatment based on these premises has been described elsewhere (Bobath, 1957, 1959, 1960, 1962, 1964, 1967, 1969,

1978). It consists of the inhibition of pathological postural reflexes combined with facilitation of righting and equilibrium reactions.

This book has been written in the hope that an analysis of the patient's abnormal motor patterns may show the cause of his manifold motor disabilities, and thus be of help with the problem of treatment.

References and Further Reading

André-Thomas (1940). *Equilibré et Equilibration.* Paris: Masson.

André-Thomas, Dargassies Saint-Anne S., Chesni Y. (1952) *Etudes Neurologiques sur le Nouveau—Né et le Jeune Nourisson.* Paris: Masson.

André-Thomas, Dargassies Saint-Anne S., Chesni Y. (1960). *The Neurological Examination of the Infant.* Clinics in Developmental Medicine No. 1. London: The Spastics Society and William Heinemann Medical Books.

Bernstein N. (1967). *The Co-ordination and Regulation of Movements,* p. 111. London: Pergamon Press.

Bobath B. (1967). The very early treatment of cerebral palsy. *Dev. Med. Child Neurol;* **9** No. 4: 373–90.

Bobath B. (1969). The treatment of neuromuscular disorders by improving patterns of co-ordination. *Physiotherapy;* January.

Bobath B., Bobath K. (1957). Control of motor function in the treatment of cerebral palsy. *Physiotherapy;* October.

Bobath B., Bobath K. (1962). An analysis of the development of standing and walking patterns in patients with cerebral palsy. *Physiotherapy;* June.

Bobath B., Bobath K. (1964). The facilitation of normal postural reactions and movements in the treatment of cerebral palsy. *Physiotherapy;* August.

Bobath B., Bobath K. (1978). *Motor Development in the Different Types of Cerebral Palsy.* London: William Heinemann Medical Books.

Bobath K. (1959). The neuropathology of cerebral palsy and its importance in treatment and diagnosis. *Cerebral Palsy Bulletin;* **1** No. 8: 13–33.

Bobath K. (1959). The effect of treatment by reflex-inhibition and facilitation of movement in cerebral palsy. *Folio, Psych. Neurol. Neuroch. Neerlandica;* **62** No. 5.

Bobath K. (1960). The nature of the paresis in cerebral palsy. In *Child Neurology and Cerebral Palsy.* Oxford: Spastic Society Study Group.

Bobath K. (1969). *The Motor Deficit in Patients with Cerebral Palsy.* Clinics in Developmental Medicine No. 23. London: The Spastics Society and William Heinemann Medical Books.

Bobath K. (1980). *A Neurophysiological Basis for the Treatment of Cerebral Palsy.* Clinics in Developmental Medicine No. 75. London: The Spastics Society and William Heinemann Medical Books.

Brazelton T. B. (1974). *Neonatal Behavioural Assessment Scale.* Clinics in Developmental Medicine No. 50. London: The Spastics Society and William Heinemann Medical Books.

Brock, S., Wechsler J. S. (1927). Loss of righting reflexes in man. *Arch. Neurol. Psychiat*; **77**: 14, 15.

Burns, Y. R., Bullock M. I. (1980). Sensory and motor development of preterm babies. *Aust. J. Physiother*; **26**: 229–42.

Byers R. K. (1938). Tonic neck reflexes in children. *Amer. J. Dis. Child*; **55**, No. 4: 703.

Caesar P. (1979). *Postural Behaviour in Newborn Infants.* Philadelphia: Lippincott.

Capute A. J. (1979). Identifying cerebral palsy in infancy through study of primitive-reflex profiles. *Pediat. Ann*; **8**: 10.

Capute A. J., Accardo P., Vining E., Rubenstein J., Harryman S. (1978). *Primitive Reflex Profile.* Monograph in *Developmental Paediatrics*, Vol. 1. Baltimore: University Park Press.

Critchely M. (1954). Discussion on volitional movement. *Proc. Roy. Soc. Med*; **47**: 593.

Dargassies Saint-Anne S. (1972). Neurodevelopmental symptoms during the first year of life. *Dev. Med. Child Neurol*; **14**: 235–46.

Dargassies Saint-Anne S. (1977). *Neurological Development in the Full-Term and Premature Neonate.* Amsterdam: Elsevier.

Egan D. F., Illingworth R. S., MacKeith R. C. (1969). *Developmental Screening 0 to 5 years.* Clinics in Developmental Medicine No. 30. London: The Spastics Society and William Heinemann Medical Books.

Fiorentino Mary R. (1973). *Reflex Testing Methods for Evaluating CNS Development*, 2nd edn., pp. 9–33. London: Charles Thomas.

Flehmig I. (1970). Neurologische Untersuchungen zur Frueherkennung zerebraler Bewegungsstoerungen bei sogenannten Risikokindern. *Materia Medica Nordmark*; **22/6**: 340–54.

Fog E., Fog M. (1963). Cerebral inhibition examined by associated movements. In *Minimal Cerebral Dysfunction.* Clinics in Developmental Medicine No. 10, p. 52. London: The Spastics Society and William Heinemann Medical Books.

Foley J., Cookson M., Zappella M. (1964). The placing and supporting reactions in cerebral palsy. *J. Ment. Def. Res*; **Vol. 8**, part 1.

Fulton J. K. (1951). *Physiology of the Nervous System*, pp. 115–32. Oxford: Oxford University Press.

Galant S. (1917). *Der Rueckgratreflex*. Basel: University Dissertation.

Gesell A. (1941). *The First Five Years*, p. 19. London: Methuen & Co.

Gesell, A., Amatruda C. S. (1949). *Developmental Diagnosis*, p. 33. London: Paul B. Hoeber.

Hirt S. H. (1967). The tonic neck reflex mechanism in the normal human adult. *Amer. J. Phys. Med*; **46**: 362–9.

Illingworth R. S. (1960). *The Development of the Infant and Young Child*. Edinburgh, London: E & S Livingstone.

Kinnier Wilson S. A. (1925). The Croonian lectures on some disorders of motility and muscle tone. *Lancet*; July 4.

Knupfer H., Rathke F. (1982). *Diagnostische und Therapeutische Praxis bei Spastischen Laehmungen*, pp. 3–78. Stuttgart, New York: Thieme.

Koeng E. (1962). Fruehdiagnose cerebraler Laehmungen. In *Diagnose und Therapie cerebraler Laehmungen im Kindesalter*, Teil I, pp. 37–44. Basel (Schweiz), New York: S. Karger.

MacKeith R. C. (1964). The primary walking response and its facilitation by passive extension of the head. *Acta Paediat*; **17**, Suppl. No. 6.

Magnus R. (1924). *Koerperstellung*, p. 75. Berlin: Julius Springer.

Magnus R. (1926). Some results of studies in the physiology of posture. *Lancet*; **Sept**: 531–5, 585.

McGraw M. B. (1963). *The Neuromuscular Maturation of the Human Infant*. New York, London: Hafna Publishing.

Matthias H. H. (1966). *Untersuchungstechnik und Diagnose der infantilen Zerebral Parese im Saeuglings und Kindesalter*, pp. 18–45. Stuttgart: Georg Thieme.

Milani-Comparetti A., Gidoni E. A. (1967). Pattern analysis of motor development and its disorders. *Dev. Med. Child. Neurol*; **9**: 625–30.

Milani-Comparetti A., Giodoni E. A. (1967). Routine development examination in normal and retarded children. *Dev. Med. Child Neurol*; **9**: 631–8.

Paine R. S., Oppé E. T. (1966). *Neurological Examination of Children*. Clinics in Developmental Medicine Vol. 20/21, p. 192. London: The Spastics Society and William Heinemann Medical Books.

Peiper A. (1961). *Die Eigenart der kindlichen Hirntaetigkeit*, pp. 155–294. Leipzig: Georg Thieme.

Peiper A. (1963). *Cerebral Function in Infancy and Childhood*. New York: Consultants Bureau Enterprises Inc; London: Pitman Medical.

Pollock L. J., Davis L. (1927). Studies in decerebration. *Arch. Neurol. Psychiat*; **17**: 20–2.

Rademaker G. G. J. (1935). *Réactions Labyrinthiques et Equilibre*. Paris: Masson.

Riddoch G., Buzzard E. (1921). Reflex movements and postural reactions in quadriplegia and hemiplegia. *Brain*; **44**: 452–3.

Schaltenbrand G. (1925). Normale Bewegungs und Lagereaktionen bei Kindern. *Dtsch. Z. Nervenheilk*; **87**: 23.

Schaltenbrand G. (1926). Ueber die Entwicklung des menschlichen Aufstehens und dessen Stoerugen bei Nervenkrankheiten. *Dtsch Z. Nervenheilk*; **89**: 82.

Schaltenbrand G. (1927). The development of human motility and motor disturbances. *Arch. Neurol. Psychiat*; 270–8.

Sherrington Ch. S. (1939). *Selected Writings* (Brown D., ed.), pp. 175–6. London: Hamish Hamilton Medical Books.

Sherrington Ch. S. (1947). *The Integrative Action of the Nervous System*, pp. 67–9. Cambridge: Cambridge University Press.

Scherzer A. L., Tscharnuter I. (1982). *Early Diagnosis and Therapy in Cerebral Palsy*, pp. 33–42. New York, Basel: Marcel Dekker.

Smith S. L., Gossman M. R., Canan B. C. (1982). Selected primitive reflexes in children with cerebral palsy. *Phys. Ther*; **62** No. 8: 1115–20.

Vlach V., Prechtl H., Bermuth H. von. (1969). State dependency of exteroceptive skin reflexes in newborn infants. *Dev. Med. Child Neurol*; **11**: 353.

Vojta V. (1981). *Die zerebralen Bewegungsstoerungen im Saeuglingsalter Fruehdiagnose und Fruehtherapie*, pp. 21–51. Stuttgart: Ferdinand Enke.

Walshe F. M. R. (1923). On certain tonic or postural reflexes in hemiplegia with special reference to the so-called associated movements. *Brain*; **Part 1, 46**: 2, 14, 16–23.

Walshe F. M. R. (1946). *On the Contribution of Clinical Study to the Physiology of the Cerebral Cortex*. The Victor Horsley Memorial Lecture, pp. 18. Edinburgh: E & S Livingstone.

Weisz St. (1938). Studies in equilibrium reaction. *J. Nerv. Ment. Dis*; **88**: 153, 160–2.

Zador J. (1938). *Les Réactions d'Equilibre chez l'Homme*. Paris: Masson.

Index